Saddle
Sisterhood

Equestrian Adventuresses
Book One

Krystal Kelly

COPYRIGHT INFORMATION

Equestrian Adventuresses Book 1: Saddles & Sisterhood

Copyright © 2020 by Krystal Kelly.

For all the future adventuresses of the world...

Go get 'em.

Table of Contents

Preface
Welcome to the Equestrian Adventuresses Tribe!

Thank you for being a part of this wonderful adventure. Putting together a collection of stories from women who speak a variety of languages and have traveled far and wide on horseback hasn't been easy. We've featured women's amazing true stories throughout this series, including adventuresses from Poland, Belgium, Australia, the USA, the UK, New Zealand, Germany, and many others. Their inspiring stories have taken us to places such as Georgia, India, Mongolia, Italy, Canada, South Africa, Namibia, Romania, Greenland, Chile, Argentina, and Bhutan.

In no other equestrian book series has so many international readers and riders come together in one place and I am very excited to say that because of these stories' young girls in Yemen, India, and others can be taken to faraway places on horseback and be inspired and encouraged to follow their dreams.

Having spent more than a decade working with horses in male-dominated countries where women are not allowed to ride, this book series has been a dream come true for me. When I was a little girl, unable to afford riding lessons or a horse of my own, I would lose myself in books and stories of girls riding horses and having adventures. I told myself that one day I would be surrounded by horses and it was because of books like these that fueled my ambitions into one day turning into a reality.

These pages contain true stories. Many of the authors do not speak English as a first language. Although we did our best to edit the stories and translate their words, a few minor mistakes here and there are expected for a big project and undertaking such as this. But the stories are what counts and these women didn't hold back! They bravely take us to unexplored lands, trail blaze new paths, and journey across exotic destinations, all from atop a horse.

I hope you enjoy each and every one of their stories as much as I have and remember to share this book with as many of your friends and future adventuresses as possible! You never know which story might spark the hidden flame that enables someone's life to change forever. I hope these tales empower future girls and women around the globe to saddle up, head for the horizon, and see where they end up.

"My heart belongs to the arena but my soul belongs to the trail." -Anonymous

Yours Truly,
Krystal Kelly

Founder of Equestrian Adventuresses
www.EquestrianAdventuresses.com

DOWNLOAD YOUR FREE TRAVEL GUIDE FOR EQUESTRIANS E-BOOKS TODAY!

www.EquestrianAdventuresses.com

In this Book Series you will find:
- Stables Listings of Horse-Riding Tour Operators in the USA and Worldwide
- Information and travel tips for a variety of countries including sights to see, highlights not to miss, and much more
- Resources to plan your ideal horse-riding vacation based on your budget, riding level/discipline, time of year, terrain, accommodation, and weather preferences
- 70+ Job Ideas on how to work internationally with horses
- Tips and tools how you can work abroad with horses as a volunteer or as a paid position and career

And much, much more!

To find our free e-books simply visit:
www.EquestrianAdventuresses.com

How Did I End Up in Bhutan?

BY SANDRA KELLY

As I sit at the Kathmandu airport, I am sweating, the air is very heavy. The room is full and the seats are dirty. I see some employees bring in a few large bottles of water to the front of the room and many of the other traveler's swarm to the water and finish it before I can even move from the row that I am sitting in. This is an airport that I am just enduring to get to my destination. I have been in many small airports around the world, but this one is one that I am glad to be leaving and trying not to think about returning to. My motivation and excitement to be here is because I am finally going to Bhutan to ride horses in a remote part of the Himalayan mountains! As a woman in my fifties who did not spend time riding horses, trail riding in Bhutan was an endeavor that had not been a known dream for me, until...

My story begins as a child in the suburbs of California. I was one of those girls that fell in love with horses upon seeing the first one. My parents gave me a technical book about horses when I expressed my desire to someday have one. I assume this book was supposed to make me forget this desire, but instead, I studied horse anatomy, breeds, and how to care for them. We moved to the mountains when I turned eleven and I hoped that would be my chance as there was a stable in a nearby valley that had a few horses. My hope was crushed by my parents not having money for lessons, the stable closing down, and there not being any place for me to get any part-time work.

Later, in my senior year of high school, I finally had an opportunity to take a few lessons and I thought for sure that horses would be in my life now. However, during college, I only went riding a couple of times. On one occasion after college, my fiancé agreed to go riding with me. We were in Georgia at the time and I found a place that let us take the horses out on our own. I went trotting off down the trail, it was a beautiful spring day, everything was green and I could smell the flowers lining the trail. Some large trees were covering the hillside and I was so happy that I was with someone that would not only become my husband but would be my best friend to ride with and spend time outdoors. What I did not know was that he was not behind me! He had trotted off in the opposite direction somewhere and it took me over an hour to find him. Needless to say, he decided that day that we were never going riding again. This did not feel right to me, but I thought, *well he will change his mind someday.*

Life went on though and I found myself too busy with marriage, working full time as well as raising two children. One child, my daughter Krystal, was very excited about animals wherever we went. This was influenced by me since the primary places I liked to take the kids were wild-life safari parks and farms.

When she was two years old, I had taken her to visit my parents and stopped at a park that had pony rides in a circle for children. The look on her face and in her eyes was priceless. Pure joy exuded from her. Throughout her childhood, she focused on horses as the main priority in her life. I was not going to discourage her as my parents had done to me, other than the practical parts of having to save to eventually have one and the importance of learning everything about them. She began taking riding lessons at nine years of age.

Krystal learned everything she could through books when she could not be with horses. All of the motivation came from her. I helped in paying for what lessons I could, but when she turned twelve her father and I divorced and I was the main income earner, so I had a lot on my plate. Krystal was steadfast though and began her first job working at a breeding stable. She saved all of her money to buy her first horse and proceeded to continue training as a showjumper and to train this huge thoroughbred that everyone was afraid of to be her everything horse. This horse almost killed her a few times, but she continued even more determined. I could see that he was her best friend and the bond between them was very strong. Tragically, he became very ill and she spent months trying to help him and all of her money trying to get professionals to help, but they could not. This was a great loss and a turning point for her. I did not know how she would utilize her love for horses, but I could see the fire in her eyes. I wished that I had her clarity, endurance, and motivation to go for what I wanted when I was her age.

Krystal continued with many equestrian programs around the country and then attended an all-equestrian college. She spent her free time working as a groom for the teachers so she could help pay for her education. Krystal tried to teach me some riding skills and concepts through all of this, but I guess I felt my time had passed and I settled for watching her through the years. I did not think I could afford this hobby for myself. I knew she would be doing something in her life with horses, however, I had no idea how she was going to make a living with it. Then one day she calls me from her school and tells me they don't have anything that she wants in their career book and she did extensive research on her own. She then proceeds to tell me that she found an internship with an Olympic rider in Belgium and she wants to go. Wow! I then realized that her world and mine were going to change. I was so proud of her for all the hard work she had done to get to that point and in shock that my now young woman was going to Europe!

For five years I went to visit Krystal wherever she worked with horses, always far away of course. This was where the travel addiction began. I visited her in Egypt, Romania, and India. Each time she would let me ride a horse and most of the time I was filming her during her show jumping competitions. Watching all of these beautiful horses and how advanced she had become over the years had further ingrained in my mind that I could never be able to ride and bond with horses to have them want to ride with me! I loved the friendship Krystal and I were developing, but I was only an observant of her world.

At that point, I was traveling more and more to visit and we did some exploring to other countries like France, Greece, Spain, and Thailand and I really enjoyed the experiences. All my other travels with my new husband were of the "vacationing-type," planned out carefully, and providing all the comforts and luxuries imaginable in our budget. These types of vacations are nice as a break from work, but how much can you truly relax in a week or two while having to travel to get there and back?

December 2015

"I finally did it! I'm retired now!" I'm flying to Indonesia to begin a two-and-a-half-month journey. Krystal had been on hiatus from her last project in Egypt and had been traveling around several countries in South East Asia. She met up with me in Bali where we planned to begin our adventures together. I am worn out from working for many years in a stressful career counseling criminal youth and then supervising criminals getting out of prison as a law enforcement agent for the last ten years. I don't know how I am going to deal with a mostly unplanned journey throughout Indonesia, Malaysia, and Taiwan...

Two weeks in, and I am feeling more motivated and capable. Today, we decided after our excursion to the Komodo Islands yesterday, that we are going to the country of Timor Leste, after all, it is the island right next to the Island of Flores which we are on right now, how difficult can that be?

Timor Leste is an island in Indonesia with a complicated history. The west half of the island is still occupied by Indonesia. The other half of the island, the east side, is its own country. It was recognized as a country by the U.N. not long ago, in 2002. Timor West (the Indonesian side) was once occupied by the Dutch, and the Eastside, Timor Leste, had been occupied by the

Portuguese. Needless to say, there was a lot of complex history involved, something we discovered more and more as we traveled deeper into the unknown.

It had been five days since we started our journey to Timor Leste, I can't even comprehend some of the setbacks and hard work that we have overcome to try getting a visa into the tiny island nation. Not to mention the difficulties in organizing transportation to take us across the Indonesia portion of the country to get to the border...apparently "tourists" don't go to Timor Leste overland.

Krystal and I are getting our picture taken with a group of the Indonesia border guards while we wait to get our passports stamped to leave the country. It is a cool, wet morning and we are on foot with our bags. I'm still having to deal with this damn rolling bag that I thought we could store in Bali until we return there for our yoga training course, but that did not happen. *Note to self, pack super light from now on.*

This huge puddle lay before me after we finally get stamped and I give a young man a few rupees to carry my bag across it. "Why not?" I say as Krystal laughs at me while walking across with her one little backpack. Well, we are at the border now. Time for me to drag my large, oversized suitcase. I realize how comical I must look to the locals watching our every move. We walk across a bridge, look up at the sign, to our left is the ocean and to the right is a steep mountain. We finally reach the Timor Leste border and find out that they are an hour difference in time and we must wait to get processed. Welcome to Timor Leste! This process was a strange series of lines and places to pay various fees. I'm already having a strange feeling about this country.

Finally, we are on the other side. There is nothing here! Except for two young boys with tiny Vespas sitting by a tree. Hmmm...luckily Krystal is a skilled negotiator. We jump on the small mopeds with them, my driver struggling to drive with my large suitcase between his legs and the handlebars. We are on our way up the winding roads to the only place for a foreigner to stay on this side of the country...an old Portuguese fort that was converted into a hotel with hardly any visitors. *And here we go...*

Two months later, after many strange and wonderful adventures, we are at a Temple in Taiwan for the Chinese New Year. As I light the incense, look around the courtyard, see my daughter in prayer, I am feeling so full of life, hope, gratitude, and joy that I overcame so many fears and have developed a traveling sisterhood with my courageous and talented daughter. I know I can do so much more now.

February 2019

Each year since I have joined her and eventually her husband joined us on some great adventures. However, I had yet to go riding on horseback in the wild somewhere, anywhere. I kept watching and hearing about the various places I was missing out on and when I heard that Krystal was filming an Equestrian Adventuresses documentary in the Himalayan mountains of Bhutan with the stable that she had trained herself five years prior, it hit me! Bhutan is said to be one of the most beautiful and happiest countries on Earth and right before me arose a rare opportunity to ride on a horse for six days in the Himalayan mountains. What the hell was I waiting for? I knew in my soul I desperately wanted to go. There was just one problem though....

I am afraid I do not have the skills, stamina, and courage to ride on mountain trails and my daughter is surprised to hear that I want to join the group. Krystal instructs me that I have to take lessons in my local area and be able to perform a list of things required for trails. The last item is to be able to canter safely.

I live in Colorado, it is winter here in February. Spring does not happen until May, the ride is June 1st. What am I going to do? Reach out to the other Adventuresses on Facebook, that's what. One woman responded and I found someone that does trail rides in the Rocky

Mountains and had a horse for me to train on. It is Western riding, but I want to get my confidence back and focus on groundwork. The weather won't allow me to start until April, no pressure, right?

I begin going several times a week and working on the ground with this huge, but very smart horse called Flynn. I'm feeling out of shape physically but good about my partnership with Flynn and I'm doing well at setting boundaries with him. Now it is time to start the re-training, I call it, in the saddle. Trotting and taking Flynn over and around obstacles is great. I am feeling pressured though that I need to step up and get to cantering. This is where my fear is trying to take over. I keep at it though.

Today is the day, I am at the point of having to decide on my own when to canter instead of being told when. I start trotting in a counter-clockwise position and for some reason, signal Flynn to canter, right before a left turn. Wow, this is the wrong choice! Flynn followed my cue, and then turned sharply, I lost my right stirrup, lost my balance and bounced up and over to the left, spinning through the air like a top, but did not let go of the reins until I bounced on the ground hitting my right buttock and then hitting my head on the ground, only to find myself sitting and stunned. Flynn was stunned as well. He stood there wondering why I did that. After a moment of shock, I got back onto Flynn and took him around a couple more times until I realized I could not do it anymore.

I realized at that point that I may have a serious injury. Luckily my husband was there, had seen what he described as a very graceful and well-landed fall. I was very lucky in that the x-rays showed no breaks or fractures, but I needed to give it some time to heal. I had less than a month to be ready for Bhutan! There was no way I was going to miss Bhutan and absolutely no way I was going to miss riding through the Himalayan mountains with my daughter and her husband. I was doing it no matter what. I bought a sheepskin pad for me to sit on, took Epsom salt baths, did yoga, took the anti-inflammatory medications, and ran through my mind all the scenarios I could think of and how I would deal with them. Having other women on Facebook that overcame many obstacles in their lives and were riding around the world on horses was my inspiration.

Kathmandu Airport.

We are finally being shuffled into another room before departure. This room is small, but it had air conditioning! Things are improving already. Finally, we get to go to the plane. As we walk across the tarmac to climb the stairs into our plane, I admire the Dragon painted on the tail end of the plane. I feel a sense of adventure already coming over me, or is it just in my head? I have no idea what this flight will be like, after many travels and planes, I had lost that sense of wonder. I never get window seats anymore because the accessibility to the toilet became more important. But today, as I was climbing the stairs and getting settled in, I was starting to wonder, was this view going to be something I will remember forever?

I am sitting with a German lady, Anna, also on our riding adventure, and as we fly along, we realize that the Himalayan mountains keep going and going and although we can't see too much on this day, we suddenly realize the surmountable skills that we are assured our pilots have. The few clouds break away to reveal a deep but narrow valley below. We look at each other and ask, where are we landing? As we look out the window, we see the side of a mountain appearing to be no more than 20 yards from the wing of the plane! I feel like I am on a roller coaster ride as we tilt left then right to navigate through this narrow ravine. Finally, I see a sliver of a very short runway ahead. Oh no, we are landing here? Anna and I look at one another then return to our new obsession of watching the outside world we are now entering, the anxiety and thrilling excitement are all I can focus on. I am amazed at how well the pilots are maneuvering the plane. We land on the ground and I stare out the window, I start to get nervous as we are approaching the end of the runway. Then we stop right on the line at the end of the runway. Amazing. Whew! I breathe a big sigh of relief.

Paro, Bhutan

The four of us now walk into the beautiful, tiny airport of Paro, Bhutan. As we had our visas handled before arrival the passport control seems very simple. This is a good sign. Our hosts are waiting for us at the door, I feel like a welcome guest visiting family. I remark about the skill of the pilots and our host states, "There are only eight pilots allowed to fly into and out of this airport, it is very dangerous and they are the only ones that are trusted to do it." Wow, maybe it was good that I did not know that before. Bhutan is one of the most dangerous airports in the world for pilots to land. I'm not surprised. But then again, where else can you fly with a view of Mount Everest, as we had done?

As we drive along the valley to our first two nights of lodging, I am finally feeling relaxed and a sense of peace. I am in the moment and glad to watch the serene landscape, small town and farms dotted along the way. I do not see any signs of chaos or stress anywhere. The surrounding mountains are very steep with a few rolling hills in the valley.

As we approach the tiny bridge that covers a sleepy stream, our host and guide Sonjay points to the mountain ahead of us and says, "We begin there tomorrow for our climb on foot to the highest temple in Bhutan, the famous Tiger's Nest Temple!" My sense of peace is now being pushed away by excitement and anxiety over the long journey we will be taking. I have heard of people getting elevation sickness as it is 15,000 feet high! I live at 5,000 feet so I reassure myself that this will help me to not get altitude sickness and besides I have a plan to be the turtle, slow and steady, and deep breathing as much as I can. That will work, it has to.

The next morning, we head out to the entrance of the trail to the Tigers Nest. I am surprised that many people are arriving as well and the majority of them are from India. Many are going to be taking donkeys and ponies up to the halfway point where the donkeys cannot go any further. We are walking the entire route. Of course, Krystal and her husband Christian are up in front, Anne, Sonjay, and I are mostly walking together, but all I am focused on is taking slow steady steps and breathing. I am having moments of having to stop and catch my breath before continuing, trying not to think of how long or far I must go, just to enjoy nature, watch out for the donkeys coming up beside us, and breathe. Two hours later, I see the Buddhist flags strung across some poles and a prayer wheel. This signifies the end of the donkeys on the trail and the halfway point.

A little farther up is the lunch hall where there is a buffet set up, tea, and water that can be purchased. We aren't having lunch yet though, this is for the return. Now we are having tea. For the first time, I gaze up the mountain in the distance and can see the Tigers Nest Temple for the first time, still high on the mountainside. I can also see some very steep stairs that we will have to take to get to it. I hope this tea gives me some more strength and helps to relieve some of the burning starting to develop in my thighs. At 54 and having a few more pounds than I should—okay, twenty pounds more than I should—I am feeling like a turtle with an extra little turtle on my shell. I am an active person, I used to be very athletic, but I do not normally hike up steep mountains for several hours each day, so this is a challenge that I am feeling proud to have completed thus far.

We head out once again, the dirt path is getting steeper, winding around the different obstacles and it is very important to pay attention to where I am stepping. I see a couple of the same groups of families that have been traversing this trail all morning with us. Small children and some grandparents as well. The goal that I now tell myself is that I must stay in front of the grandparents.

Winding through the mountainside it is feeling a little cooler and the views are intermittently showing the vast expanse of the valley and surrounding mountains. It's quite a lovely day to be doing this hike. Finally reaching the stairs, I am relieved that it is a sign we are drawing near to the Temple but anxious as I start to climb them. Oh my, these aren't stairs! These are a variety of ladder-type stairs and frightening uneven blocks of narrow stone and cement that thankfully have a metal handrail on most of them. Sonjay reveals that the hand railing is new. So, my daughter had done this years ago before they put the railing on "for the tourists." Wow... I'm glad I didn't visit my daughter the first time she came to Bhutan to work with horses.

This is tough. My thighs are burning, the air is very thin, and the cliff next to us is very steep. I glance over toward our destination occasionally and think *I'm coming, I will be there soon enough.* Sonjay reaches his hand out to me while I had paused for a moment to breathe and I declined stating that I must do it at my own pace. He understands and just stays near me, watching over me like a guardian. He goes back to his own loud deep breathes with an exhale that includes a deep sound. I feel comfort in knowing that even a younger man who is physically fit—and probably has done this hike a million times—must focus on his breath as well.

Finally arriving at the entrance to the Tigers Nest Temple an hour and a half later, I am feeling so happy to have accomplished this journey and realize it is not over yet. We still have many stairs to go up and down as we venture through and learn about the intriguing history of this great temple. As I gaze out at the distance with Krystal, I see parts of the stairs, trails, the vast valley, and mountains and I am feeling connected to the world and her. What a wonderful opportunity to share this experience with my daughter. Now I am feeling more confident that I can traverse the mountains with a mighty Bhutanese horse.

The trek down has its challenges, there are still stairs to go back up that we descended to get across a ravine before arriving here. We finally get back to the lunch building and have a simple but needed buffet lunch. Tonight, I will rest for sure.

Once back at our rooms and having the Chinese buffet the hotel served us for dinner, I get to my room to rest. I'm having some stomach issues. But I have some medication to take that seems to help. In the morning we are up at 5:30 to get to the airport. We have to fly to the other side of the country for our horse trek. We have one problem though, Anna is very ill. I am sure it was from the food that also affected me, but I am wondering why I am not so ill. I feel terrible for her and I am not feeling that great either, but we are flying and just getting to the Homestay today. Anna is determined though and gets herself together for the trip, the excitement of seeing the horses too great to miss out on.

Bumthang, Bhutan

Up in the air again for another masterful and amazing flight, this time we all made sure we were in line first to get window seats. Today is an up-close look at the Himalayan mountains in Bhutan! Clouds interspersed the view, but I am in a trance the entire 30-minute flight, just gazing at the mountains, valleys, small villages, large rivers, and crops. Such a beautiful country. We finally arrive at the valley of the town Bumthang, with an even smaller airport. I see a small building as we are landing, the size of a small house with a viewing tower on top of it. Our luggage is brought to us with a small cart that was driven through the grass by a small tractor to where we were waiting next to our tour van. Such hospitality!

We are taken to a nearby hotel for a rest and lunch. Anna and I were given rooms to rest in as we were both tired. After lunch, we take the long drive into the mountains to our homestead. There is a beautiful river next to the home and from my room, I can see the valley and river below. It's a very simple room that was occupied by a few spider roommates. Well, I'm camping in the mountains starting tomorrow, so these roommates have their own little web at least.

After lunch, we go to meet the horses. The ranch is quite remote on a hillside at the edge of the forest. I meet my horse, Tashi. His name means, good auspices or good luck in the Bhutanese language. I certainly hope the name fits well. He is a follower and does not want to be left behind by his spunky friends. Krystal watches me and gives some helpful tips for my riding and position on the horse. I am so glad to have her wisdom and a watchful eye to make sure I am prepared for the trails ahead. This is her third trip to Bhutan and she is very familiar with the horses and trails as it was her that had come to Bhutan to help develop the riding program!

We take a ride up the hill and are surprised by a team of baby pigs running as fast as they can to catch up to the adults. Wow, they can run fast, and they are so tiny! This is a good start. As we trot along the road, I realize that my injury is flaring up some, but the short canters are so smooth feeling on this mighty little horse. I love the feel of this!

As I go to bed for the evening, I begin to feel quite nauseous. Then it began, vomiting and diarrhea. Hour after hour. To make it worse, the toilet seat in the bathroom fell off! It is finally morning and I am so weak. I tell my daughter that I can't move. To my surprise, Sonjay arrives with the owner of the Homestay and states that he is a retired doctor. I am comforted to know my blood pressure is fine and I do not have a fever. He gives me some crackers and rice to eat and I rest for a few hours. I awake to them telling me that they have gotten the horses ready and rode them to the beginning of the trail and if we leave now, we can make it to meet them. I am not alone, Christian was not feeling well also. Always nice to not be alone. I muster my strength together because I am not going to miss this adventure. I came too far for this. I feel a little better and just won't push myself too much, just stay at the back of the pack and keep it slow and steady. Sound familiar?

Himalayan Mountains

I see the group and my horse waiting for us ahead, I am so glad to see my sheepskin pad on the saddle. It somehow brings me comfort. If I weren't so weak, I would be jumping for joy right now, I am on the trail with my daughter and her husband for the first time and I get to be a part of a horse-riding adventure and not just looking at pictures and videos. Tashi has a nice stride and my sheepskin is comfy, but as we walk along, I am feeling the pain on the right side of my tailbone and still feeling very weak and dizzy. As we climb up the mountain, I am relieved some that it feels better than on flat spaces. Through my delirious state, I cannot think much and I just start gazing at the beautiful terrain. The fluorescent greens of the grasses and ferns are mesmerizing. There are so many different types of plants and some very rare flowers that are still in bloom from the spring. Tashi is like a mountain goat climbing up and down rocks, through narrow trails. I have to stay alert to adjust for the steep terrain and wild branches coming at me. This is not a well-blazed trail, but the horses know it well. As we climb, we go into the clouds and the moisture turns into some light rain, though it's more of a heavy fog that engulfs you with moisture than actual rain.

I am glad that the man that cares for the horses daily, Lhamo is staying at the rear with me to keep Tashi from running with his friends. I am not ready today for that. I try a few canters, but the dizziness takes over. As we approach the area close to where we will camp for the night, there is one last steep climb to the top of the mountain where our tents are. There is not a real a path so we are climbing through these dense bushes until alas, we are at the top.

I am so exhausted I just climb into my tent enough to pull out my sleeping bag and sit for a moment until Sonjay arrives with some rice and a few crackers. I take a few bites, then lay back to fall into a deep sleep. Somehow in the middle of the night, I awake. I see my boots are still on and sticking out of the end of my tent. I grab my flashlight and decide it is time to find the toilet tent. As I emerge outside the fog is so dense, I can barely see the other tents next to me. Mine is located at the end with nothing but ferns and forest in the distance. I quickly find the tent and scramble back to my tent and finally remove my boots. I suddenly remember that there are tigers in these mountains and we are at 10,000 feet above the sea. That is a high mountain for me. I'm sure the horses will let us know if any come around, so I should be fine. I drift back to sleep in the silence of the forest, going back into the deep sleep that I need.

Morning arrives with a very pleasant view that I had not noticed the night before. My fern grove outside of my tent opened up to a view of the valley below and the surrounding mountains. The colors are so surreal. Everything is wet and I just want to hurry up, get a small breakfast, get ready, and get back to riding. I am feeling better now and don't want to miss the world we are in. We ride on the ridge to go visit a local Monastery. We are very lucky that Sonjay had studied to be a monk when he was young and he proceeds to tell us the history and some of the stories of the Monastery. The deep reverence for the Buddhist religion and nature is emanating from the philosophies he shares with us.

We return to our horses and I am feeling focused and connected to where I am and with my family. I have always loved the mountains, this place feels alive and I am happy to be on a horse, sharing the sights and sounds with everyone and just being here.

We ride back down this mountain with the view of the valley ahead of us, some small farms along the way have cute baby donkey's playing in their field on this beautiful day. We ascend another mountain to arrive at a flattened future build site that tonight will be our campsite. Nearby is another Monastery that is full of boys that are in training to become monks. Sonjay encourages Christian to drive the old work truck used to bring in our supplies and transport us over to the Monastery to visit the temple. This is an adventure of its own on this narrow, muddy, and twisting road, but lots of fun!

As we approach the Monastery there are different groups of boys playing with sticks and rocks. The older boys are sitting on a bench listening to some music and trying to look cool. We enter the temple and Sonjay continues with another piece to the story and history of his country. I am listening to him as I look at the painted pictures on the walls that give a visual of the story. I can picture the rest in my mind. As we walk back to our campsite, I take in the vast view these young monks see every day. Surely it must inspire them as it is for me as I wander back.

After dinner, I am feeling ready to rest. During the night the local cows wandered throughout our camp and in the morning, I found a present outside my door from them. They liked rubbing up against my tent and left me a cow pie. Oh well, maybe it is good luck.

Today we are going to the valley and I am looking forward to more open spaces to ride on. Cantering along these mountain trails is still a little scary for me. Everyone else is loving them though. A small marshy valley is ahead and I see a wooden makeshift walkway wandering through the marsh. This is a narrow path, but I am glad it is here, the mud and grass along the edge look very deep if the horse steps into it. As we traverse this walkway, I am glad my recent training focused on navigating obstacles with the horse. Another mission accomplished.

Wandering through the valley through some villages and farms, it is relaxing and wonderful to see life being lived by the locals. They are hard-working people with a calm reserve. We come across a remote valley with a long expanse for cantering. Everyone decides to race to the other side. I wait for the rest to go then I go for it! I am using some of the breathing and techniques that Krystal taught me, I am feeling so in sync with Tashi, his gait in canter just flowing in this comfortable but exhilarating speed. The speed increases almost to a gallop and for the first time in my life I feel how wonderful it is, as I come up to the group, I can't help myself as I yell out ecstatically, "I did it!"

I see Christian laughing with joy as I ride past. I feel like a child that just rode my bike for the first time on my own. This sounds silly, but I am so excited to know that I can do it, I have had the knowledge but not the courage to allow myself to progress before. Now I know I will be going on more horse-riding adventures with my daughter and I finally feel a connection and understanding of why horses have always been and will always be a big part of her life. Krystal sees the joy in my eyes and on my face and in that moment without saying anything we know that this is a great moment in life. One that I will cherish forever.

Now I know what kind of horse I am connected to as well. I have ridden various breeds and they were beautiful but did not feel like Tashi. Some people may love to experience the various types of breeds, but I have discovered that for now, this size and shape of a horse is great for me to explore mountains and wildlife on. The local Bhutanese horses are rather small, pony-sized, and more like "Mongolian horses," Krystal tells me. But it is clear that these sturdy horses thrive in the mountains, their sure-footedness never ceasing to impress me.

The next couple of nights we are staying at farmhouses with local families. I am enjoying riding and learning about the culture. I see elderly people that spend their day at the temples walking around the outdoor prayer wheels. The humble attitude they present is comforting as they gather together and encourage one another during the rest breaks. As they sit to have the lunch they brought for the day, I feel like the choice they have made to spend the day together at a place that brings them peace to be a positive way to spend the day. We ride on to the river where a table has been set up for our lunch. The large almost flat granite rocks make for a great spot to sit on the edge of the water and gaze at the scenery while listening to the water rushing down between the rocks. I am reminded of my youth when I spent a lot of time sitting next to mountain rivers enjoying the day and just being happy.

The wind picks up and some sprinkles start to fall upon us and we must finish this lovely respite time. Onward to our homestay. Tomorrow is going to be the longest day of riding and the most difficult terrain. I am feeling some anxiety as I wonder what that will be like. We will have to climb up a ravine to a mountain pass that is almost 10,000 feet high. I am told the climb is steep. I reassure myself that I am capable and I know that Tashi is a very sturdy mountain horse that has done this trail before. I dose off with the memories of streams and ferns to ease my anxiety.

This morning I am trying to make sure I am prepared for the long day ahead. I look forward to getting to the pass where the Buddhist flags mark the top of the pass. Ascending the trail starts fine, it is a beautiful morning. It takes a couple of hours to reach the ravine. This is like climbing a terraced waterfall, luckily without all of the water. There is some water trickling down and I just hope it does not rain or this will not be possible. Tashi climbs onto some of the boulders almost slipping, I am so glad he is sure-footed. I do what I can to keep my weight balanced for him.

The slow-going climb through the ravine reveals an ancient forest that has a mysterious aura. This is enhanced by the steam that creates pockets of mist as the sun rises. I am mesmerized by the old-growth trees that are disfigured from the elements over the years. The rocks, ferns, plants, birds chirping, and wind in the trees make for an engulfing experience. This is as deep into the forest one needs to go to feel connected with nature. The hours go by. Sonjay instructs us to dismount as we must climb to the peak of the pass. I see the flags ahead and try to take a deep breath in the thin air and take in the moment. Krystal, Christian, and I have some fun taking pictures of us with our horses to celebrate this accomplishment. I truly appreciate Tashi for bringing me up here.

For the descent on the other side, we are on foot until we get past the steep trail that has a deep muddy ditch. The horses will be released to follow us on their own. I try to safely, but quickly make the descent because I am at the back and I know the horses will come up behind me. I almost made it to the bottom of the trail before I saw the horses barreling down the path, I step aside off of the trail to let them through. They know what they are doing and stop at the bottom.

Now we are continuing down the mountain and I see a hillside meadow ahead. To my dismay, I see the bones of two horses that were taken by tigers over the winter. This reminds me of finding deer carcasses in the mountains at home that had been taken by mountain lions. Only Tigers are so much bigger.

I look up toward the tree line that separates the high mountain from the meadow and see where the Tigers must have been waiting for their prey. Yes, this is as wild as it can get, I think. Venturing on we come to the village of Lhamo, our riding companion who doesn't speak any English but is graceful in the saddle and has a natural way with the horses that is mesmerizing. His village sits high on a hill with meadows all around and the immense mountains in the background. Such a beautiful yet rugged area.

The end is drawing near and we take advantage of the open spaces to get some cantering in. The rest of the group decide to have a full-on race and I gladly volunteer to take a video of them, not quite ready to experience galloping just yet. Seeing the joy in Christian and Krystal's eyes as they take off across the open field brings me a lot of happiness. The ranch is ahead and we say our goodbyes to Lhamo and the crew that took such good care of us. I will miss Tashi and thank him for being such a great partner for the past six days.

Krystal and I walk over to see the mother horse that lives on the ranch with a young foal. I feel connected to her now in a different way than ever before. Through all of our travels together, having this experience with the passion of her soul is a connection that could never have happened if I had continued to just watch from a distance. We don't have to discuss anything, she just looks at me and asks, already knowing the answer, "How did you like this riding trek?"

I smiled and replied, "I loved it, even more than you know." The look on her face showed the wisdom I used to see in my mother's eyes and I knew she felt the same.

Run Like the Wind

BY JEANNETTE POLOWSKI

When you think of The Bronx, which is New York City's best borough, (in my not so humble opinion) ... I'm going to bet that the last thing you think about is horses! I also highly doubt you would think of beaches, either. But when I remember my youth, horses and the beach are among my favorite memories. I think of growing up in an Italian ghetto, near the Bronx Zoo, where I would hear the sounds of the wild animals drift up and in through my open windows. Seals bark, very distinctly, and exotic birds make the oddest warbling sounds.

Orchard Beach was where we went to cool off on hot summer days. I would squeeze onto hot, overcrowded buses with my friends, and we then would lurch and bump our way along, to go have fun in the hot sand and cool water. It was crazy how sometimes we waited for what seemed like an eternity, only to have three overcrowded busses in a row pull up. Sometimes kids would steal bus rides by hanging onto the back bumper, where the bus driver couldn't see them. I've always assumed they didn't want to be sardined inside, with the boom boxes already playing loud salsa tunes and the smell of coconut suntan lotion permeating the air.

The 20 minutes or so ride usually seemed twice as long and when the doors opened, we all pushed for freedom like it was a fourth of July fireworks explosion—loud and colorful. It was then onward, stepping out to the crown jewel of The Bronx, the gorgeous crescent-shaped beach created by Robert Moses in the 1930s. For us, though, the beach also had an additional lure. When the weather cooled, and the crowds disappeared, we looked to the beach as a pretend desert to be raced on by our swift horses, and the water's edge represented the closest thing to a manicured, professional horse racing track that we could imagine.

When I was a child, I would sometimes ponder the randomness of life. I would wonder about why some kids are born into royalty, others on a cattle ranch in Montana, and yet others live in a vast urban setting...like I did, in The Bronx. I thought it was a cruel injustice that I was fated to live in a concrete jungle when all I ever longed for was wide open spaces and horses at my disposal. How unfair was it that I couldn't just wake up, go saddle up my mount, and ride out onto the range surrounded by nature? I thought it was terribly unfair, and I used the Bronx Zoo to ease my inner pain. I often had my grandmother, Coco, take me there on a free day. Lots of times I had her take half of the kids on the block with us, after all, it was better than being cooped up in an apartment or hanging around on our street.

My Grandfather was a barber in our neighborhood. Every man and boy around got their hair cut at Chief Cuts, which he owned. He was also an avid gambler on the ponies, otherwise known as Thoroughbred Horse Racing, the Sport of Kings. Because he loved to bet on them, he frequently went to the track. Belmont Raceway was my favorite, and I went with him as often as I possibly could. He would do his betting thing, and I would run down to the paddock area before each race and observe every horse. I was somewhat familiar with the main trainers and jockeys, so I looked at the horses and sized up their odds of winning in my head. I had a pretty good system figured out. I considered multiple factors, such as the size of the horse compared to the distance of the race, and whether they were running their race before they got onto the track, or if they were calm and levelheaded.

Now, honestly, I did take trainers and jockeys into account, but not as much as my gut feelings about each horse. I occasionally imagined that I would see my favorite racehorse ever born, Man o' War. I saw his giant, chestnut muscles flexing as he prepared for his races in the paddock area, dancing and prancing by me on his way out to the starting line. How I LOVED him! I would usually take some time out of every day to look at a painting of that majestic stallion on my living room wall. He was my sports hero, and I was sad he had lived before my time. Even though I never personally got to pick my beloved Man o" War to win, my overall win percentage was pretty good. I fancied myself to be a savvy non-gambler!

In these young days, I was not yet a rider, but I dreamed of it while I was sleeping AND awake! The burning desire in my heart was so strong that sometimes it manifested itself as actual physical pain. Now, I know that this is hard to believe, but as it turned out, The Bronx was home to multiple horse stables. It was the highlight of my days when I could catch a glimpse of a rider on horseback, or groups of them, trotting down the trails, riders bobbing up and down. The riding trails were carved out in various places alongside many busy roads, so if I was in the right location, viewing was assured. My favorite barn to pass was at the end of a service road to a busy parkway. It was a dead-end to cars, but not to me! To me, it was where I began riding horses.

Bronx Riding Academy was my refuge. It was a place that took me away to another world, another life, another reality. There I could be the real me and immerse myself in horses. I could escape the concrete by swapping it out for dirt and sawdust. I could take out groups of riders and pretend that I was herding cattle instead of people, while I wrangled them up and down long dusty trails. I laughed at the mental images and loved every minute of it.

It was at Bronx Riding Academy that I met and made lifetime friends. I had finally found kindred souls who also felt lost in the cityscape we found ourselves in. Our mutual escape zone was a large concrete barn that was built into a hillside. Because of this geography, there were 2 levels where horses were kept. The very upper third level was a meeting room/locker, room/office. The lower barn was where the "Hack" horses lived, and the middle level, upper barn, was home to some of the "Private" horses. The remaining "Privates" lived behind the barn in a large converted tractor-trailer beds made into box stalls. They had half doors for the day-time and sliding doors with locks for when we closed at night. The trailers lined the perimeter of the backyard and formed a courtyard of sorts, which kept you from seeing and going near the high-speed train tracks that formed the rear end of the property.

At our barn, we also had a large sandy arena, otherwise known as The Ring, which was short for riding ring. It was located at the far end of the barn and extended towards the common bridle path, where fellow riders from other stables could pass by or come on over to visit us. Three popular riding academies shared the system, so we used these trail as if they were highways. It was possible to get to and from all the local barns, of which each one had a distinct personality. The paths were meticulously maintained because they were part of the New York City Parks Department. In some areas, the trails were twenty feet wide, while in other spots it narrowed to a mere 3 feet. Each riding academy had access; they were all interconnected.

I found myself spending every waking moment at Bronx's. I would wake up, shower, and take off! I'd run down the street, hop on a city bus, and be transported to my horse haven. For quite a while, I worked at the stable in exchange for free riding privileges. We didn't have a lot of money, so that was just fine with me. Riding for free meant much more to me than any salary. I reasoned that this tradeoff enabled me to ride more than I ever would have been able to afford, anyway. But I still longed for a horse of my own.

One gorgeous day, I was pushing a wheelbarrow full of hay to the top barn when I noticed the truck from Buck's Horse Trading making its way slowly down the service road, towards Bronx's. Buck was a well know guy. He found and sold horses to be used for both business and pleasure to all of the barns in the region. Knowing this made me burst with anticipation because this meant we were getting some new horses in! I couldn't get that wheelbarrow up the ramp and feed those private horses fast enough. All I could think about was investigating the new arrivals. I practically threw the hay biscuits at the startled animals.

As I turned the corner from the barn to the parking lot, I saw a dapple-gray gelding being led down a ramp onto the pavement. This was the moment that I first saw my beloved Grey Ghost. I fell in love with him right there, on the spot. We locked eyes as he lifted his head and took in his new surroundings. His intelligence radiated from deep within those dark pools, and I loved his ears. They were outlined in black and accented his face perfectly. His mane and tail were black, laced with silver. I let my eyes wander over every inch of him, and I appreciated everything about him. He looked to be a thoroughbred cross, of sorts. He was of lean build, and stood about 15.2 hands, with high withers and chiseled legs. His legs were banded in black and ended at dark, large hooves. As I stood there, time had stopped, and I gently reminded myself to breathe.

After that day, he became mine. No one knew a thing about his past. He was estimated to be about 19 years old based on the length of his teeth, but he sure acted like a yearling! When I was on the ground around him, he was calm and playful. I could walk under his belly while currying him, and he never even batted an eyelash. But, as soon as you put your foot in the stirrup, he was 1,000-plus pounds of forward motion! Riding him was what I imagined it must be like to ride a cat.

He was agile and fast. It took me quite a long time to get him to flat walk in the company of others. The first time I ever took him out of the ring, I rode out on the trails with some friends. He crow hopped, danced, and pranced in every direction. He had such high knee action, drawing his front legs up incredibly high with each step. He had a soft, responsive mouth and tons of pent up energy. I thought of the track horses I had seen so many times, as he was soon covered in white lather, just like them.

On a whim, and maybe just because I was tired of restraining him, I gave him his head and leaned forward at the beginning of a long flat stretch of the bridle path. Ghost exploded from underneath me. The power of his forward thrust took me by such surprise that I popped out of my western saddle and found myself sitting behind it. As I climbed my way back into my proper position in the saddle's seat, the wind was whipping my hair and eyes. We were going so fast that tears were streaming down my face. Despite this incredible display of speed and power, he was acutely aware of me on his back. As soon as I touched the reins and asked him to slow, Ghost did so, like a perfect gentleman. I was awestruck, humbled, and exhilarated all at the same time.

Word soon spread. Everyone was talking about Jeannette and Grey Ghost. Nelson, one of my dear friends, came up with an idea. He proposed that we take Ghost back out onto the trail where there was a wide straightaway, and then, another one of our friends, Ralph, would drive his car on that same stretch of the parkway. I was to give Ghost his head to run freely, and Ralph would stay shoulder to shoulder with me, for that stretch, and clock our speed with his car's speedometer. I was on board right away with the plan. I honestly didn't have any other way to answer my burning question, exactly how fast was Ghost?

The stretch that we chose to clock his speed was located directly across the south side of the parkway, where Bronx Riding Academy was located. This was great because we had an audience. It was also determined that Carla would accompany Ralph to ensure he clocked the speed correctly. Carla was a tough cookie, and we knew she'd keep him honest!

I took Ghost to the starting point and simply dropped my reins and leaned forward. He took off, and without one ounce of urging from me, he flew across the dusty surface. That horse experienced a sense of joy from running, and he charged ahead full speed. Ralph gave his little car gas and kept shoulder to shoulder with me, as promised. I eased Ghost up after a nice quarter-mile run, and we turned back for the barn to meet up with Nelson, Ralph, Carla, and the others. We arrived greeted by great fanfare! Grey Ghost had cruised to an easy speed of 45 miles an hour! To put this into perspective, according to The Guinness Book of World Records, the fastest speed ever recorded for a racehorse over a 2-furlong distance was almost 44 mph. The great Secretariat topped out at 49 mph. My Grey Ghost truly had the speed of champions!

Grey Ghost now had some serious street credits among our local riders, from all of the barns. Word traveled quickly, and I enjoyed the feedback from people who looked at him, and us, with a touch of envy. He was gorgeous, flashy, and fast! A guy who was interested in owning a horse at Bronx's even pulled his truck off of the parkway right onto the riding path and offered to give me 5 thousand dollars cash on the spot, if, of course, I would sell Ghost to him. I declined.

I loved to race Ghost against other horses. If someone challenged us, I would eagerly accept. I had all the confidence in the world in our ability to win. My galloping gelding beat every horse that dared to engage us. I had a great group of friends that rode the trails with me daily, and they all knew that Ghost and I were a force to be reckoned with. We would set out on adventures throughout the area, on any given day. We ran through trails, swam in the bay, trotted down city streets to go get sandwiches from the deli, you name it, we did it.

Bronx's was, overall, a very low-key barn. Western-style riding predominantly ruled. At the far end of the trail system was City Stables, and they had a good mix of both styles. English style riding was more popular there than at any of the other local barns. I became friends with a girl there, her name was Veronica.

Veronica was around the same age as me, but she came from a very wealthy family in Manhattan. On a visit to her New York City apartment, I was shocked to see fireplaces and 10-foot-high ceilings. The unit sprawled out over an area that I'm sure was 10 times the size of the apartment I lived in. Even though Veronica came from a much different background, we were equal on our horses. The love of horses was a great equalizer among all of us young riders. Whatever we were when we were not out playing with our horses was left behind and irrelevant. What did matter was that we were horse crazy equestrians sharing our experiences in a world that we knew belonged to us, and us alone.

Veronica was an English rider, and her horse was a stunner. He was a 6-year-old registered quarter horse with racing bloodlines, named Westchester. Westie, as she called him, was quite the horse. His glistening, solid chestnut coat glowed like the embers from a fire and he was just as hot. The only white on him was the thin blaze that ran down his forehead and ended at the tip of his nose. He had powerful hindquarters and muscles that quivered with every movement. Veronica handled him perfectly. He was a strong horse, but not crazy. He was young but came to her well-schooled, if not a bit frisky.

I rode over to City Stables pretty regularly. Sometimes just Ghost and I went, and other times we had the whole Bronx Riding Academy crew come along, too. There were 10 to 15 of us, all together, from Bronx's. Veronica had a bigger barn at City Stables, and yet probably had only about 10 or so regular friends that would join us out on the trails. This was not because of any social problems; City just had more adult riders than youth.

Somehow, someway, somewhere along the line, Veronica and I started to become a little bit competitive with each other. I was a bit cocky and sure of myself, and she was used to being alpha just because she could be. We both had strong personalities, which is probably why we got along, and why we also clashed.

As the fall started arriving and the days became chilly, for some reason, and I don't know why or when exactly, people started to whisper about Grey Ghost and Westchester. They wondered who was faster. I began to catch wind of the gossip and was surprised that anyone would think that Ghost could be beaten. After all, he was proven to be "Grease Lightning." He had dusted every horse who tried to take him on. But he hadn't faced an opponent with the blue bloodlines of Westchester, whose horse racing heritage was unrivaled. I didn't worry, I had complete faith in my horse. I was, however, annoyed that my peers now seemed to question the superiority of Ghost, and I. I had the fastest horse... I just knew it. I knew his heart, his speed, his power. How could anyone else not see that he was the best?

Then it happened. Veronica and I were out riding with a large party of mutual friends, and because the crowds of beachgoers were no longer around, we found ourselves hitting the trails that led to Orchard Beach. We all stopped when we reached the sandy stretch, and as if we were all of one mind, plans for a match race began to take place. It was decided that we would run a distance of a quarter-mile, down on the hard-packed sand at the water's edge. I wanted the race to count for something more than my ego, so I proposed that we race for money. It was agreed that the winner would take home $50.00. In those days, that was a pretty good amount of money. I didn't want to make the sum too large for fear it would cause the race to be called off. By this point, I wanted to face Veronica and Westie and shut down the wagging jaws of doubt. I'd be lying if I didn't admit that a small voice in the back of my head tried to say, "What if you lose?" I tuned it out.

We set the race for two weeks from then. It was the talk of the town. Wagers were being placed and sides were being taken. I tried to prep Ghost a little by breezing him along open trails, but never allowing him to run full speed, just easy gallops to let him enjoy himself a bit and stay on his game. I tried to sit in his stall at lunch and tell him that we were going to have to prove to all of those doubters that he was the best, but in his usual fashion, he only wanted me to share my sandwich with him. Ghost didn't have a care in the world. He had no idea that our reputation was on the line.

Race day was cool, but sunny with a deep blue sky. I remember the sky in particular because there were no clouds to be seen. I took this as a good sign, but despite my best efforts, I was very nervous. At the barn, I saddled Ghost up and was surrounded by my closest allies. Dottie and Daphne were on either side of me as we started towards the dirt highway that would lead us to the proving ground. Behind us, Little Joe, Brian, Tracey, Nelson, Carla, Ralph, Artie, and his brother Stanley followed. Ronny and Wilson had gone ahead of us to stake out a good area to view the race. One that wouldn't cause any interference with the horses that were running. We didn't want any distractions. Once the race began, we wanted Ghost and Westie to only focus on each other and the task at hand.

Much to my surprise, as we approached the beach, I saw that quite a large crowd was there already. There must have been about twenty horse and rider pairs just milling around, waiting for us to arrive, while raucously debating the potential outcome of the day's event. Veronica was already there. Westchester looked as radiant as ever, and I was sure that I saw him breathing fire. Maybe it was just the smokey condensation of his warm breath, blowing out of his nostrils in the cool afternoon sun... I really couldn't tell, and my imagination was running a little wild at this point.

I told myself to get a grip, and I rode straight towards Veronica. "Hey Girl," she called out to me, as I got closer. "Today's the day," she said, with a little too much smugness for my liking.

Veronica then announced, to my astonishment, that MY friend Stanley was going to ride Westie in her place. I was so shocked I was speechless. Stanley? How could he have agreed to do this for her, and yet never say a word to me? Was she paying him to do this? I had so many questions swirling around in my head at that moment.

Veronica knew that Stanley was a skilled horseman and that he would be able to get every last bit of speed out of Westchester. It occurred to me that she was scared and that she didn't have enough guts to ride her own horse in this match race. It told me that she wanted to win, but it also showed me that she was conceding that Grey Ghost and I were a team she didn't think that SHE could beat. I also thought her move was fated to lose because I estimated that Stanley was about 40 pounds heavier than Veronica. In my opinion, it was not smart of her to add that much weight to Westie and expect him to run faster than Ghost.

I chose not to protest. I would NOT back out of the race, and there was NO way that I was going to lose to them, just no way! A deep line had been drawn in the sand to mark our starting line, and a second one marked the finish line. We sent the crowds to the viewing area and the neutral judges rode over to their places to observe both the start of the race and to officiate at the end of the race. We agreed that we would abide by what was determined by the judges. We were ready.

Ghost was hyped up by now, as he undoubtedly felt my tension coming through the reins. I thought of my many visits to the paddock area of Belmont Raceway. I didn't want Ghost to run his race before we started, so I did my best to try to send waves of calmness to him. Retrospectively,

I don't think I needed to bother. He knew what was happening, and he wanted to get out there and run his race.

Stanley hopped onto Westchester, who looked like he was ready to run. Stanley reached out his hand to me, and I took it because I decided to forgive him for riding against me. We both declared, "May the best horse win!" and rode over to the starting line.

Grey Ghost was quivering with anticipation as we began to crow hop our way over the line in the sand. Stanley positioned Westchester to my left. He was closer to the water's edge than I was, so technically this was equivalent to having the inside rail at a horse racing track. The distance was shorter the closer you rode to the curve, not by much, but every little bit helps. The tide was out, so the beach was wide, and the hard, wet sand was perfect. We were both holding our horses in, about 3 feet apart from each other. I listened for the countdown, as I readied myself for the signal to begin.

"GO!" Screamed Theo, the starting line judge.

The whole world seemed to fall away at that moment. I felt Ghost burst forward as I leaned towards his neck and thrust my hands up along his flowing mane. That first stride found us neck and neck with Westchester. That fireball of a horse had a quick start and the powerful forward thrust of a quarter horse should never be underestimated. The world was moving in slow motion to me, even though our actual speed was blistering fast. With the second stride, I watched Ghost's left eye size up Westchester, and I felt him gathering himself under me. He wasn't underestimating his competition; he was reading him like a book. That third stride was where it all ended for Westchester. Ghost propelled himself forward with a leap. He opened up his stride and flew, close to the ground and ahead of Westie. With each bound, he increased the distance between them, and we passed that finish line a few lengths ahead. We were the winners. Victory had never tasted so sweet!

I was so proud of my horse! I learned something about him that day, too. He liked to win just as much as I did. Maybe even more? I realized that I was his passenger and that I was just along for the ride. But it was because he loved and trusted me. I let him be him, and he let me share his life and loved me for it.

I was happy, the rumors were put to rest, and Veronica went back to her barn and got over it. Truthfully, we never really hung out together after that. It wasn't intentional, at least not on my part, but it just was the way it wound up being. I didn't mind, but I think things just couldn't go back to the way they were before that fateful day. We were forever changed by that collective experience. And not just us, but also the spectators and judges that were there that day. This little race was a big event and is still talked about today, almost 40 years later. Artie recently told me he was secretly hoping I would win and beat his brother Stanley.

Grey Ghost, the gorgeous dapple-gray horse of unknown background, became a legend on that day.

My Canadian Hero: An Encounter with Bears

BY DANIELLE HASLAM

Sunday

Sitting in the front seat of the pickup truck, looking out the windscreen at the jagged snow-capped mountains rearing up in the distance, it all seems rather surreal, the driver is a fishing guide from the lodge where I am going to be staying and he is talking to me very enthusiastically about all the various types of salmon that can be found in Canada.

I feel like I am drifting in and out of reality, it seems like a lifetime ago when I crept out of bed, leaving my husband sound asleep in our cozy little cottage in Yorkshire, since then I have traveled many hours and thousands of miles to arrive in British Columbia... so I decide it's ok just to drift along and let the country and western music on the radio wash over me....

A couple of hours later the pickup pulls to a halt in front of a wooden lodge nestled at the side of an azure blue lake surrounded by pine forests and mountains, the very same mountains that I had been looking at earlier in the pickup, it's breath-taking. As I slide down from the pickup feeling a bit heavy with jet lag, a handsome rusty and white dog with a huge bushy tail comes bounding up to me. I bend down to fuss him and tickle behind his furry ears "who are you? handsome boy" I ask him, as he flops at my feet "that there is Ruckus, he just loves meeting new people" I look up to see a pretty woman in a cowboy hat coming over, "hi I am Tara," she says, Tara is the head wrangler and horse trainer at the lodge. Tara proceeds to help me with my bags as I just gawk around taking it all in. Tara shows me to a cute little log cabin and advises that lunch will be served at the main lodge house in half an hour.

The cabin is so cozy, there is a comfy looking red checked snuggle chair that looks perfect for curling up with a book in, a crackling log fire, and a huge picture window, through which I see, two mares with foals grazing on a lush green lawn. Beyond the horses is dense woodland, behind which rises up a mountain topped with white. "Wow, I could spend hours just looking at that view" I whisper to myself...

At lunch Tara chats to me about the lodge and the various horses she is training and although I have traveled here alone, in Tara's company I feel welcome and at home. After lunch, I change into my riding gear and head down to the corral, I must admit I do feel slightly prim in my breeches, jodhpur boots, chaps, and riding hat, as I look at Tara heading towards me out of the barn, looking all relaxed in jeans, a checked shirt & cowboy hat. "Come on Danni let's go catch you a horse", Tara says. I feel excited as we head to the corral. Tara climbs the fence and heads into the middle of the herd. I wait, watching the mass of horse's circle, manes toss and tails flick, then moments later the herd parts and Tara is walking towards me leading a stunning chestnut horse with a white diamond at his forehead. "This is Chance", my eyes glaze over as I look at him, he is so handsome!

Back outside the barn as I groom Chance, I ask Tara about his breeding and find out he is a quarter horse and an actual cow horse! He has come to the lodge from a cattle ranch as his previous owner had too many horses. Jacques, another wrangler, wanders over to me for a chat and advises that Chance is not a novice ride and will try to cut to the front when loping... loping? I think... ah yes cantering. Chance meanwhile playfully tries to grab hold of the brush I am using with his teeth...

Just before we mount, Tara whistles, and Ruckus and a pure white wolf-like dog called Snowy, bound over. "For the bears," Tara says and goes on to explain that the dogs will bark and scare away any bears or mountain lions we come across. "Bears, mountain lions?" I gulp... at that point I realize this is not going to be like a quiet little hack around the countryside back home. On my rides at home in Yorkshire, I love encountering wildlife, but usually, the wildlife consists of shy deer and stealthy foxes that bound away from me, without needing dogs to chase them off. I swallow and look suspiciously into the trees nearby.

Once mounted, it all feels very strange, I have ridden English style for over thirty years and now suddenly I am riding along on a skinny path, with a steep fifty foot drop to the lake at the side of me, with long floppy reins, no contact and am trying to understand the concept of neck reining... Chance feels tense like a coiled spring beneath me.

We arrive at a long grassy meadow. Tara calls back that we will have a lope. Chance jumps forward, I am jolted along, I feel like I am bouncing up out of the saddle and then banging down on Chance's poor back. It feels awful, completely out of control. Chance pulls trying to get up to the front of the ride... my heart is beating fast, oh my gosh it's like I cannot ride... thankfully the lope is short, and Chance finally pulls back to a jog.

Jacques, riding at the back, has taken all of this in and notices the look on my face. He explains that as Chance was tense his head was very high, making his back hollow, which is why I was bouncing so much. He asks how much I have ridden recently and when I say that I have a horse at home and I ride four to five times a week, I register a mild look of disbelief on his face. Not surprising really as I have just ridden like a sack of potatoes.

The ride continues down past a wide fast-flowing river and with delight I notice a bald eagle looking down at me regally from a tree, we pass below him and meander through a pine forest dappled in sunlight... surrounded by nature I begin to feel chilled out and in response, I feel Chance unwind beneath me.

Our second lope goes much better. Tara comments that Chance looks more relaxed, "which is good," she says, "as we had to swap a guest off of him last week as she couldn't control him." I decide I will try to ride him the best I can. On the way back to the lodge Jacques gives me lots of helpful tips and says I can use both reins in lope to help steady Chance, so I will try that on tomorrow's ride.

That evening as the sun is setting, I look out of the window and notice a wonderful rainbow. I go outside to look at it and the inquisitive little foals wander up to nosey at me, they are so fluffy and cute, they try to nibble my clothes. I find out later they are the offspring of a wild stallion! "Lovely little accidents," Carey the lodge owner calls them. It's a magical feeling as I play with them on the lawn in the twilight.

Monday

I wake up early and feel a bit homesick. I look out of my cabin window and see the wilderness and feel quite alone... I am missing my husband... then I think of how long I have dreamed of visiting this remote place.

"Right, buck up Danni," I say out loud to myself and I wander outside to see my little foal friends and then head to the main lodge for breakfast.

I feel better after breakfast, chatting to Tara and the fishing guides that work at the lodge. As I walk down to the horse paddock, I think it's beautiful here and I decide I am going to enjoy it...

The day's ride takes us to an emerald green lake, as I ride, I feel relaxed and at one with my surroundings. I feel like I am riding Chance better and he is responding to me more. Sometimes the trail is hairy with huge drops to the side of us, but my trust in Chance is growing and over the day I begin to worry less about the footing. Loping goes better but I still need to get Chance to relax more and drop his head.

We stop for lunch at a spectacular viewpoint. I sit in the grass admiring the green lake and the craggy mountains surrounding it. Ruckus heads over for a fuss and to see if I have anything good in the sandwiches, I have just pulled from my saddlebags.

Chance is tied nearby eating grass, he looks very pleased when I wander over to him to share my lunchtime apple and we share a quiet moment as he lips it gently from my hand.

I chat to Tara as we wander back to the lodge, we exchange stories of our horse travels, she tells me of when she worked at an estancia in Chile and I tell her fondly of Paddy my gorgeous skewbald cob back home.

On the way back, we bump into Jacques who is out training one of the young horses, he tells me he is amazed how relaxed Chance looks and that I am riding him well. I thank him and inside I beam a little, as I lean forward to scratch Chance's neck.

Tuesday

Today we turn our horses in a new direction and ride downriver, through new forests. Tara tells me a fire came through this way a few years back, so in some parts, the trees are only a few feet high. On the ground the charcoaled remains of the old forest crunch under Chance's hooves. I look up to a ridge and notice a mule deer watching us, Tara informs me they are called that due to their big ears and I laugh.

We canter a lot on the ride, my favorite is one where we cut in and out of trees, I feel the agility and balance of the mighty quarter horse as Chance weaves from side to side under me, I am grinning from ear to ear as we move as one.

On a high trail, Tara pulls up and turns to me, "Would you humor me, Danni? I brought my camera and I wondered if I could take some pictures of you and Chance?" I knew Tara was a keen photographer, as we had discussed photography the previous night at dinner.

"Sure," I said, "where do you want us?" Tara instructs us to lope along a ridge. When I see the photograph a few days later it's spectacular. Tara has captured the very essence of my trip to British Columbia in one shot. In the foreground Chance is loping, Chestnut mane flying, face alert, I am on his back grinning at the camera looking relaxed. We are set against a backdrop of pine forests and in the distance are the ever-present snow-capped mountains. It's just beautiful and over the years to come, I cherish the picture and the memories it invokes.

We pull up for lunch at an abandoned cabin, I sit with Tara, with Ruckus contentedly curled up at our feet and we chat about the different ranches she has worked at and I begin to think cattle work may be fun, especially now I have seen how a cow horse can move!

A plan starts to form in my head around taking trips over the coming years staying at ranches, haciendas, and estancias from here in Canada down to Chile... A Pan-American Pony Tour... I munch my sandwich look at the river and ponder the possibilities of the horses I could ride on such a trip. Quarter horses, Appaloosas, maybe even a mustang! Peruvian Pasos, Paso Finos, Marchadors & Criollos.... *Wow, how cool would that be?* I feel giddy in my stomach just thinking about it.

On the ride home, as we make our way through some tightly packed pines, Chance moves along steadily below me and I drift along looking up at the trees. I am jolted from my peaceful daydreaming as I notice a branch snapped off to the right of us, the end is shaped like a lance and Chance is almost on top of it. I catch and hold my breath as I think it may go in Chance's side, it's too late to move over. The end of the branch comes up the saddle flap tears through my flimsy English breeches straight up the flesh of my leg. I grab the branch and heave it aside, through this I make not a sound, as I lift the branch away Chance has not even noticed. I stop and call to Tara that I have had a bit of an accident, as she stops and sees the blood running down my leg with a worried expression she says "Oh my, are you ok? How come you didn't call out or make a sound?"

"I didn't want to spook Chance," I say. "I am so glad it didn't hurt him," Tara gives me a look of approval recognizing the typical first response of equestrians the world over when an accident occurs, a concern for their horse over themselves.

We canter most of the way home, as we blast up an old airstrip, I discover a half-halt works nicely to stop Chance barreling off. I am falling a little in love with him... I love how he nuzzles my hands when I stroke his face and how curious he is of everything.

As we arrive back at the ranch Tara tells me I look bad-ass riding in my ripped breeches, then guides me to the lodge to patch me up. I make a mental note to buy jeans to ride in for future western adventures.

In the years to come, I often look at the scar as I dress for riding and think fondly of Chance and Tara.

Back at my cabin I shower and go to sit on the deck with my book.

A few minutes later, Don walks past. He is the resident bear man at the lodge. He stays year-round and is a fountain of knowledge on every-thing-bear. "Hey Danni, want to see a bear?" he calls. We walk over to the fence of the horse paddock, I am expecting to see a bear up on a ridge at a distance. What I see blows my mind, a huge blond grizzly is strolling down the paddock not fifty feet away. He is just sauntering along eating some grass, then he stops and looks at us, he looks right at me and for a moment time stops and I am looking at this wild thing and he is looking right back into me. I never thought I would see such a thing in my lifetime! Then he turns, walks on and jumps the fence at the bottom of the paddock, and heads off into the trees.

Don explains to me what to do if you meet a bear out on the trails, "If it's a grizzly, back away quietly, don't turn, don't run. If you meet a black bear be aggressive, be big, don't back away..." I ponder with interest the two different strategies for bear encounters.

Later in my cabin, I reflect on the day, amaz-ing experiences like today, riding with Tara whose life is so different to my own but with whom I feel an instant connection due to our love of horses and nature, seeing wildlife up close in its natural habitat and feeling a partner-ship with my horse are exactly what makes me travel. I know I am fortunate to have a good job, which enables me to save money to travel and I have a very understanding husband who lets me go out into the wide world and live my dreams....

I am so lucky, that bear made me feel humble, alive, and slightly scared in my stomach!

Wednesday

We head out from the ranch to undertake a ride called the roller coaster, it is a breathtaking ride. The first lope takes us through winding trees, as usual Chance and I lean from side to side, trees whipping by. Then we break from the tree line out onto a ridge with a huge steep drop on one side down to the forest floor far below. I feel my butt clench as I look down.

"Trust your horse!" Tara shouts back, "he will not allow himself to fall, he will stay on the path." I watch as loose stones from Chance's flying hooves bounce over the edge, then I take a deep breath, look forward and force myself to release the vice-like-grip I have on his reins and give Chance his head. We fly along the ridge, adrenalin pumping through my veins, "Woo hoo!" I whoop as we slide to a halt at the end of the lope. Tara is laughing, "Now that's the kind of reaction I like!" I was grinning all the way back down to the valley. At the bottom we lope again through the trees on the valley floor "it's a full six minutes of loping," Tara informs me. Chance is amazing, never slowing the whole six minutes just bounding along beneath me. I smile the whole time.

On the way back to the lodge I spot a big tan grizzly up on a ridge watching us. I chat with Tara about different types of horse training, she is going to email me details of the natural horsemanship methods her and Jacques use, so I can try them with Paddy back home.

Back in my cabin that evening, as I write in my journal I look out at the mountains across the lake, they look pink in the sunset. I replay in my mind gliding along the ridge on Chance, it truly felt like we were flying. I decide it's my favorite ride so far.

Thursday

During the night I wake to hear the rain pouring down outside and in the morning at breakfast, Tara suggests doing a boat trip today as the trails would be too wet. After breakfast we head out across the lake on Brad's boat, Brad is Carey's dad and he founded the lodge. Brad is originally from Oregon, he used to come up to the lake on fishing trips with his pop when he was a child and fell in love with the place. Years later he came back, bought some land and built the lodge, and set it up as a hunting, fishing, and horseback riding outfit.

The day looked moody with grey clouds hanging low on the mountains, which at points sprang straight up from the lakeshore. It was very choppy and as the boat rolled, so did my stomach, but I keep trying to focus on the spectacular views and not on what my breakfast was doing in my guts!

We stop up at the head of the lake to explore an abandoned cabin. Brad tells me he owns the cabin, and someone trashed it a few years back, goodness knows who as it's in the middle of nowhere and only accessible by boat. As I walk around the cabin, I get a creepy feeling that makes me shiver. I would not want to stay on my own out here. I like wild places, but this place has an awful loneliness to it.

We wander back down to the beach and Brad points out some moose tracks in the sand, I gaze down at them in wonder.

As we eat our lunch, sat on a couple of logs watching the waves gently lap the shore, Brad tells me a tale.

Years ago, he let two women stay at the cabin for a week, one of them was a writer and was drawn by the remoteness of the place. She thought it would help her writing. He dropped them off with supplies and they were all happy and smiling. A week later when he picked them up, they said nothing the whole boat ride back to the lodge, Brad thought it was strange but did not press them for an explanation. Once at the lodge they went straight to bed, the next morning when Brad's son asked them how their stay in the cabin had been, they both roared and tried to claw his face! What happened here? What sent the ladies crazy? Who trashed the place and why? I knew that place felt wrong... urgh. I was glad to be back on the boat, watching the cabin get smaller in the distance as we headed on to the other side of the lake.

At the next stop, as I climb out of the boat, my foot slips. I grab onto the railing at the edge of the boat but my feet are flailing in the air trying to find the jetty. I start to slide down the gap between the boat and the jetty, I look down into the freezing lake water, imagining going under and being trapped, down in those murky depths. Fear pulses through me and then suddenly there is Tara holding my arms and grabbing the back of my jacket pulling me back on board... we both laugh with relief as we land back on the deck. "Danni," she laughs, "I thought you were a goner, but you were clinging on like a monkey!" I thank her for acting so quickly. Giggling, I feel slightly foolish. I paid more attention to the next attempt and managed to get onto the jetty safely.

I hike with Tara, to a beautiful little cabin on a small lake. We stand side by side and look up to a glacier on the mountain across the lake and notice a waterfall trickling right down into the lake, so quiet, so peaceful...

Apart from my trip overboard, it had been a fabulous day, although it did make a good story at dinner that night in the lodge, with Tara telling everyone about me gripping on like a monkey and both of us giggling. I wandered back to my cabin hoping Chance had enjoyed his day off and wondering what adventures tomorrow would bring.

Friday

Today we set out to ride up Mount Tatlow. Standing proud at over three thousand meters (nearly 10,000 feet) Tatlow is one of the principal summits in the Chilcotin range of mountains. As we wind our way up through the trees, I savor the clean sharp smell of the pines. We stop to rest the horses in a beautiful meadow carpeted with lilac and yellow wildflowers. Chance takes the opportunity to refuel and munches away at the rich green grass. Further up, the going is hard and even my strong fit Chance is blowing hard.

"Come on lovely boy, you can do this," I whisper as I stroke his strong neck. As we come out of the tree-line the views open up. The lake is way down below us and all around us, I can see snow-topped mountain peaks. At one point on the trail, my nerves feel twitchy as we are trampling through snow and there is a long dropdown at the side of us. I trust Chance though, I know he will keep me safe. At the summit, we rest, and I sit admiring the views right across the lake through Chance's ears.

The route back down is almost as tough as the way up, it's steep, in sections we walk leading our horses. Later I am back on Chance and we are almost back down the mountain. Tara is in front of me and we are chattering away. Suddenly Ruckus stops and barks, away to the left of us is a huge black bear in the woodland. Ruckus leaps forward and runs to chase the bear away, but Snowy the other dog is behind our horses and does not follow Ruckus to back him up. The bear stands his ground and does not run away. Then he turns his great bulk towards Ruckus and charges, Ruckus panics turns tail, and starts belting down the narrow path towards us, with a quarter ton of bear chasing him.

"Hell!" I think, I look quickly around but there is no way off the trail. There is a long drop to my left and to the right the ground is too steep for Chance to climb. I cannot do a 180-degree spin as there is not enough room for Chance to turn, my heart is in my mouth. Then Tara stands up in her stirrups flings her arms out and shouts "Hey!" really loud. The bear suddenly stops ears twitching, thinking... the bear takes one long look at Tara... turns and lumbers away. phew, I let my breath out.

"Tara that's the second time you saved my hide," Tara just smiles and we laugh as Ruckus is looking at us with his tongue lolling and tail wagging like he was the one who just saved us from the big bad bear! We arrive back at the lodge shortly after safe in one piece.

Saturday

I wake up and look out the cabin window, taking in the dense woodland where the grizzly disappeared the other day. I wonder if he may still be down there looking back at me in my cabin.

I am heading home tomorrow, so for the final time, I pick up my riding hat and head down to the corral. Chance nickers as I walk over to him with his rope halter. I slip it over his nose and he nuzzles my hand gently. As I groom him that morning, I try to memorize every inch of his soft glossy chestnut coat, his strong back and quarters. Once I am mounted, we head off through the woods eager to see what delights Tara has in store for our last foray into the wilderness.

I am delighted as we head out on the roller coaster ride again. This time as Chance and I fly along the narrow ridge there is no doubt in my mind that he will slip or stumble. I don't look down at the ravine as my strong brave horse lopes beneath me, instead, I look to the sky and smile...

We arrive at the old airstrip where we take up the lope and instead of Chance tearing off, he canters nice and collected. He carries his head wonderfully relaxed, I sit comfortably and move with him, whispering to him how gorgeous and courageous he is, his ears twitch listening to my voice. We have come such a long way together since Sunday.

As I pull up at the end of the airstrip I say to Tara, "I think maybe Chance is tired, he was so collected on that canter."

Tara smiles at me and replies, "It's because you ride him so well."

I feel happy inside as I lean forward to pat Chance's muscular neck. Then Tara tells me I am the first guest ever to ride Chance for the full week, so some of our trails he was seeing for the very first time. I feel such a sense of achievement, I have learned so much from Chance, and learning to ride him well has boosted my confidence.

At the lunch stop, Ruckus curls up close to me and I rub his furry head, I thank Tara for such an incredible week.

"It's been an absolute pleasure, Danni, I have really enjoyed our rides and it's been so great to see Chance doing so well," Tara replies.

I head over to Chance to share our last apple and as I stroke his head, he regards me with his gentle brown eyes, and I sneak in a little kiss goodbye. I know I will miss him so much.

In the afternoon we ride on the opposite side of the lake. Tara notices the fishing guides coming over to meet us in the boat. Tara turns to me and says, "Let's lope and look cool." I laugh and we lope down a long flowing path to the lakeshore, with me grinning wildly... although I am not sure I look as cool as Tara.

We dismount at the lake where the fishing guides have arrived with the boat to take us back across to the lodge. Tara explains the horses will swim across, however, Chance has never crossed before so he will have to be on a long lead rope attached to the boat. Tara turns the pretty grey mare she has been riding loose but instead of going into the lake, the mare spins and bolts back up the trail. Tara is a bit worried as we saw bear tracks back that way, she goes back up the trail and tells me to go ahead and cross in the boat.

I climb on board and Ruckus jumps in and settles down next to me. Chance is tied to the back of the boat, as the boat moves forward slowly, poor Chance's face looks more and more alarmed as he walks into ever deeper water. I call out encouragement to him, telling him to be brave, he snorts, then grimaces and starts to swim steadily along, nose held high out of the water. Once on the opposite bank, Chance wades out. I remove his halter and watch as he gallops away free to go join the herd. I turn to see Tara's mare step out of the lake, shake vigorously like a dog and then tear off after Chance.

The boat heads back across the lake and returns with Tara, she climbs out sopping wet. She had led her mare right into the water as the horse was spooking at something and Tara wanted to calm her and make sure she crossed ok and didn't get stranded on the opposite side of the lake. As she strolls up the lawn carrying a saddle, I look at her and think she is my hero, the type of horsewoman I want to be.

That night as I sit in my cabin and take in the view of the wilderness for the last time I reflect. I have been in Canada for one week, but it feels like I have been here in this beautiful, tranquil place much longer. I feel relaxed, I have had so many amazing experiences, my riding has developed, and I feel I have built a great partnership with Chance. I smile as I think of Tara, the conversations and laughs we have had as we spent hours riding across this wild landscape.

Then I look up to the mountain and chuckle as I ask it, "Where shall I venture next on my Pan-Americas Pony Tour?"

Adventuress Genes

BY CISKA VANDENHAUTE

Adventure is in my genes. I have always had incredible women in my family, however, my grandmother – on my mom's side – is the one I am most amazed by at times. She is the only true adventuress in our family and has led the most remarkable life. Before she got married and gave birth to my mom and my aunts, she used to roam the seven seas and travel on a quest to see every country in the world.

When I was a child, I would always ask about the many stories she knew how to tell so eloquently. Every time she told one, I felt as if I was right there with her. The way she spoke of her adventures would always guide me through the many countries she had traveled to. I loved hearing tales of how she sailed on a huge cargo ship, which she boarded in the Antwerp harbor because she didn't have enough money to travel in a passenger's ship. While out on the sea, she met a beautiful Polish captain. Every time she tells me about it, I feel like I can still see the pain in her eyes from having to let him go afterward.

Another favorite story of mine was her grand adventures with Icelandic sheep, which frightened me every time she spoke about it. She had visited Iceland on her own when she was about 21 years old and one day decided to go out for a walk on the trail on the fairy-tale-like, rocky lands. This was during the nineteen-fifties and my grandmother didn't have any smartphone or GPS to guide her back. She got lost pretty quickly. She didn't bring a map either, though I always wondered but never asked if she was simply too proud to take one. When she found herself lost in this unknown landscape, she stumbled upon a flock of sheep who were crossing an ice-cold, but a small river. Guided by these sheep, she managed to find her way back to the civilized world.

Growing up, my grandmother would take me on countless trips to Italy, a country of culture and food, and that's when I inherited her love for flying and traveling as much as I can. She fell in love with Paris decades ago and took me every time she could, so my taste for culture is deeply ingrained.

I am the kind of girl who grew up on a small farm in the Flemish countryside in Belgium, in a small town not very far from the historical city of Ghent. Our house was in a thinly inhabited street and our neighbors could be counted on one hand. I lived there with my mother, father, and my two younger brothers. It was a calm, loving neighborhood where everyone knew one another and where my brothers and I grew up freely and happily.

We had a huge garden and meadows, all at the back of our house, where we would play for countless hours. In summer, our garden looked like Southern France with the green weeping willow growing in the middle of our lawn at the back of our house. During winter, on the day's everything would freeze over, our house and the garden had a fairy-like white coat that we were almost afraid to touch. We sheltered two horses, a big rabbit, and his rabbit family, a guardian dog, and lots of mice in the stables. They knew very well how to build a warm nest in the stray of the horse's beds, in the wood that my dad would split and store in the large shed he built for the stables, the food, and his old little tractor that served many years as our meadow maintainer.

My mom has been a horse fanatic her whole life and she managed to pass the addiction onto me. Surrounded by animals, and my parent's love for horses, made me climb on the back of my sweet pony for the first time.

One of our two horses was my mom's very fierce black mare named Caresse, which is French for "gentle stroke,". This was a very poorly chosen name because she would chase away every living creature that would dare enter her meadow. That is, except for my beautiful grey Welsh pony named Pimpernel. She had a beautiful grey coat, with the lower part of her legs black. When the horses would walk in the meadow across the street, people would sometimes stop and ask my dad if she was for sale – which she wasn't, obviously!

Pimpernel was a lovely pony, however, she wasn't trained very much. What a wild thing. She was not ideal for a child learning how to ride, but I started anyway when I was about 7 or 8 years old.

My mom taught me how to ride, but that was no easy task. Countless falls and fails later, I finally managed to stay on this dear little pony. When I was 12, I had grown too big for her and my parents bought me a small horse. He was a very friendly gelding, but without known bloodlines, so we had no idea about his roots. However, we did notice that he was part thoroughbred, because of his character, delicate nose, head, and legs. Meanwhile, my mom rode a big Belgian Warmblood, who was constantly scared by his own shadow and who would make different airborne pirouettes when he spooked.

Together, my mom, myself, the nervous thoroughbred, and the very scared Belgian Warmblood, regularly went riding on trails in the surroundings of the place we lived. Although we lived in the countryside, we did have to use asphalt roads most of the time. A big part of our rides consisted of angrily yelling at kamikaze drivers on the road and jumping in the wells next to the street to prevent ignorant drivers from running us over. Doing so with two horses who loved to scare the hell out of each other when there was nothing to see but ghosts, was an art form.

My little horse was the sweetest boy and I rode him whenever I could. This included: bareback riding and him bucking me off every time I tried to ride him bareback, him running away every chance he could while I tried to get him from the pasture, and me trying to jump over a slide I "recycled"—stole—from our garden. I also avidly remember being bitten whilst playing in the field, along with my ego who got bitten too, pretty hard actually. And falls countless falls. It's amazing how I've never broken anything on that dastardly—I mean sweet—little thing.

One time, I brought him to a summer camp at a barn not far from our house. We tried trotting some jumps and to keep my horse from galloping (and to teach me how to keep my horse from galloping), my trainer put one pole on the ground in front of the small jump I was supposed to take. Needless to say, my horse jumped all the poles together and after two or three of these gracious jumps, I fell. Hard. On the sand, fortunately. Bless that arena.

It was horses and the love for them that brought my parents together, but this didn't appear to be enough. After years of a seemingly happy marriage, my parents divorced. At the time, it seemed very out of the blue since my brothers and I had always been raised in a very loving environment. It came as the worst surprise in the world. The divorce shattered my life into pieces and I felt alone in a world which now seemed split in two.

Arrangements had to be made, as is the case in every divorce, and my mom decided she could no longer work on our small farm alone. She put our beloved house for sale and even before the ad was published, it was sold to another family. She sold my horse too and moved her Belgian Warmblood into paid stables not far from where we used to live.

We moved into a different house in roughly the same neighborhood and fortunately not too far from where my dad now lived. After everything changed, it felt like a thunderstorm had ripped my life apart and everything I had ever known was now destroyed. It was a different house, with no dad around, and no horse to ride.

This was when my mom and I didn't get along very well. I couldn't ride anymore and our new garden was much smaller than the one I grew up in. It felt like only mom was to blame. Although I lived with her, I refused to do my chores or help out in the garden, as this didn't feel like it was my home. Eventually, I moved in with my boyfriend and I didn't see my mom that often, creating a distance not just emotionally, but physically as well. It seemed like the distance between us would remain, perhaps even grow wider and wider as time went on. The risk of losing one another felt very real and something needed to change.

Then one day my mom reminded me about a promise she made me when I graduated high school: that someday, we would go riding in France, in the Camargue region where wild horses run free in the wide meadows and in the swampy area. At first, I wasn't too convinced this trip would take place. We still weren't getting along and because of everything that had happened between us, I didn't trust her enthusiasm. But mom was determined to make the trip happen.

She proposed we go to the big yearly horse expo that takes place in Ghent, where she was sure we would find our answers. After all, neither of us knew how to plan for such an adventure and needed some guidance. Curiosity got the best of me and I went with her. We discovered to our delight, different travel agencies offering what we were looking for, and we started our quest for the perfect horse-riding trip in France. It wasn't until I saw the wonderful pictures of a Camargue horse hanging on one of the stalls at the expo that all my fears and doubts went away... Alright, let's do this!

The trail would go from Lubéron, part of The Provence region, all the way down to Saintes-Maries-De-La-Mer, a lovely village in the Camargue region and the coast of Southern France, not very far from Montpellier. Mom and I went by train, which is much easier to use for travel from Belgium and a lot better for the environment. We arrived in Marseilles, in a huge open spaced railway station bathing in sunlight. Weather in Belgium hadn't been that nice, since it was already October, but in Marseille, it felt like we were reloading our daily dose of sunlight.

We were told someone would come to pick us up and when we rolled our trolleys outside, we quickly noticed an older man holding a signboard with our names written on it. He helped us place our luggage in the suspicious, old-looking minivan he drove and the moment he opened his mouth to start talking, mom and I had to listen more carefully than we had ever done. What a thick Southern French accent! Mom and I are both fluent French speakers, but this one was a little over our heads. We had lots to practice in the following days! The other guests spoke either French or English and since my mom and I speak Dutch as a first language, we had a lot of fun enjoying that the other riders couldn't understand us. It happened to be the first inevitable sign of our bond rebuilding.

After picking up some other riders, we finally arrived at our guesthouse. Now, if there is one thing we should have known about Southern France, it's that its people are not known to be the most "hygienic folk" in the world. My grandmother had already warned us and indeed, at our arrival in the guest house, we immediately noticed she was right. The bathroom was tiny and damp, as were our beds and I'm pretty sure I saw something moving during that first night—it was not my mom's feet, I can sure as hell tell you that.

Fortunately, we would only sleep here during the first and last night of our trip because the trail would lead us to different parts of the south and thus to different bed and breakfasts or "gîtes," as they call it in France. During the first evening, we were asked to have dinner and appetizers with the other riders and the guide in a central dining room. As we entered this cozy area with the rustic interior, I immediately felt at home. We sat down at the big dinner table where everyone gathered and it dawned on me that mom and I weren't the only ones who had this passion. Our lifestyle is international! There were three other British women and one Swiss man, who knew the agency very well as he already was a friend to the guide and the owner of the agency. While we got to know each other a bit more, we all enjoyed a typical French dinner with bread, cheese, and "pot au feu." And of course, lots of white wine which helped to facilitate the conversations with this worldly group of strangers.

The next day, we got to know our guide who looked very much like a French cowboy. He was a local guy, who had worked as a guide in many parts of France, including the north. He rode a small Camargue horse, named Monsieur Marcel and who would later turn out to be a real show stealer!

We met the horses at their stables as they were already waiting for us to tack them up. I admit I was skeptical at first because the way our guide assigned the horses to the riders was a bit peculiar: we had to line up before him and he only asked us whether we had experience or not. Then, he took a quick look at us and wrote down the name of our horse in this little notebook he carried around and that was that. All aboard! The horse he put me on was rather small but with long elegant legs, 4 hard hooves that were accustomed to the southern soil, stubborn but very beautiful with a peculiar set of colors. His name was Thunderson, which was not an easy name to pronounce for my French guide. My mom got an even smaller, grey horse who listened to the name Sentenza. The other horses were bigger and there was one adorable little Haflinger who would join the herd.

After tacking up and getting to know the horses, we mounted up, and off we went. While everyone mounted their horses, I noticed some of the other riders had difficulties doing so, which made me feel a bit more confident since I didn't have a hard time climbing on top of my Thunderson. Maybe I hadn't lost my touch after all...

We started our first ride through the many vineyards in the region and I immediately felt like I could trust this horse. He was a sure-footed gelding who knew where he was going and who was very familiar with the track we were following. This turned out to be a great discovery since we had to cross a wild river... well, in my mom's and my eyes. It was called the Colorado River and our guide urged us not to look down while crossing the rapids. At first, I was curious why we shouldn't, as I had no experience crossing rivers on a horse. However, I was soon convinced by the guide's well-meant advice: when you cross a river with a lot of currents while looking down, it's like reading a book in a moving car, only worse. Your eyes get two completely different signals because you walk straight, while the water below you is going to the right (in our case), so you get dizzy and feel nauseated pretty quickly. So, day one and already two lessons learned: the horse knows where to put his feet, and the guide is always right. Check.

Over the next few days, I remembered why this trip had been such a big dream of mine. We climbed the Alpilles, which is like an introduction to the Alps, and enjoyed the most amazing views of France I had ever seen. At the top, we were not nearly as high as the Alps but had a breathtaking overview of the Alpilles and the villages below. Together with the clear blue sky and the horse's ears in front of us, I knew this was a moment never to forget.

Mom and I were riding side by side, in the front closest to the guide so we had the first glimpse of everything new which came around every corner. I could feel the ice melting between us, with every step our horses took and with every exclamation of admiration for the astonishing view. France started to take over our hearts and I was reminded again of my grandmother, the original adventuress of the family.

As wonderful as the Alpilles were, we had to cross them in 2 days and we moved on to a completely different landscape: the Camargue, land of swamps, and wild horses. Being the trip's final destination, mom and I immediately knew this was the reason we had come. Although we had seen some of France's most astonishing landscapes, the Camargue turned out to be next-level beautiful. We entered a combination of sand, dunes, and swamps – not the dirty, stinky, smelly green waters you would associate with swamps, but clear water-like 'little seas' on a green beach. We walked through enormous puddles of clear salty water, sometimes for more than 20 minutes. Our quest led through various meadows, that were often closed by a gate we had to open and close again, to prevent the bulls grazing in the meadows from escaping. These bulls are typical for the region and as the Camargue is not very far from Spain, the bulls are part of roughly the same culture as the Spanish toreadors. We never had the pleasure to meet one of them, not that we wanted to.

As the swamp area ended, the dunes disappeared and we walked up a beach to the Mediterranean Sea. We let the horses roam freely and walked next to each other. The weather was amazing, not too warm, not too cold, and a slightly warm breeze caressed our horse's manes. Suddenly, our guide shouted a warning for a trot and before I knew what was happening, Thunderson took a giant leap and started what was to be the fastest canter of my entire life. Even after these five tiring days full of trots, canters, and climbing, my horse still had enough fuel for a buck or two. We galloped along the sea and I saw my mom in front of me on this tiny horse, running at the speed of light. At that moment, I felt like I could take over the world on my speedy little horse. We had the perfect ending to our dream holiday and I did it all with my mom by my side.

While on this trip, I noticed how much my mom and I are alike. I never noticed it until our French adventure, but whenever we stopped for lunch or dinner, mom and I were the ones eating and drinking desperately, trying to restock our fuel for the next day's escapades. We had the perfect bathing schedule for the room we shared and whenever we could enjoy a buffet, we would reach for the same food. We laughed at each other's jokes and it felt like it had been such a long time since we'd shared these precious moments of happiness again.

After our France experience, it became clear that we didn't want to let our newfound discovery and love for equestrian travel end here. After a few months, we contacted the same travel agency and asked for another trip within Europe that would suit us. One trip drew our attention immediately. It was in a wonderful location, with challenging and beautiful weather. And so, we booked our second adventure together, which would again take place in October. As the months were passing by, the memories from our French adventure started to fade and I noticed I began reaching out more and more for the pictures I had taken in France, to be able to revive the memories more and more. I hoped for the same experience in our new destination and couldn't wait for us to get on that plane and leave.

We arrived in what must have been the smallest airport I have ever been in and got picked up by the hotel owner. She had parked her car in the middle of the road while we put our luggage in the trunk and got in without anyone hurrying or worrying about the street situation we were in. This van didn't seem quite as old as the one in France though, and I felt somewhat relieved.

I noticed that the city we arrived in, Heraklion, on the island of Crete, was very busy, colorful, and full of lights, but in a very old-fashioned way which I found rather charming. There were to be no skyscrapers, no big towers, and no fancy stores. The buildings alongside the road were mostly painted with the bright blue color people would associate with the Greek culture and their flag. As we drove further away from the city and closer to the hotel, the colors started to fade away and they disappeared into the brown, rocky landscape of the Cretan mountains. The car huffed and puffed higher up the mountain and finally ascended a steep, non-asphalted road. Our arrival at the hotel couldn't be more like a fairy-tale: blue sky, a view of the island as far as the eye can see, an outside kitchen, and an infinity pool.

By the time we met the other riders, the sun disappeared behind the horizon and I started to feel my eyes getting heavier. However, we couldn't go to sleep as there was a group of ten other women to meet. At first, I felt a little reluctant to participate in riding with such a big group, as I have always preferred a smaller number of riders. But as it turned out, my fears were unnecessary. This big group was full of remarkable international women!

Later on, when we finally climbed into our beds after a real Greek dinner, I wondered how I could have ever doubted this. I talked with the owner of the hotel and found out she has led one of the most interesting lives I have ever heard.

She is a Dutch woman who came to Greece in her younger years to work as a horse-riding guide for tourists. She didn't plan to stay but fell in love with a Cretan man who had the same dream she had: starting a tourist business on the island. They started from scratch and built the hotel we were staying in starting with noting, into this wonderful building, with an arena offering the most astonishing view ever, and stables for the horses she had imported from The Netherlands. Her mother also came to Greece and now lives not far from the island. She and her husband, the man she fell in love with all those years ago, have two children. They are wonderful little ladies who speak Dutch, Greek, and English. I nearly fell off the chair I was sitting on and told her how I admired this life path she had chosen. What a woman!

The next day, in light of there being so many women, I learned that the joke was merely on the guide: who was a man. He was the only man in our group and even though at first, I felt sorry for him not being accompanied by other men, I quickly noticed he knew his way with the ladies. I didn't know if it was the fact that he came from Eastern Europe or the fact that all these women surrounding him gave him a lot more energy, but he sure didn't have any problems entertaining us. Not that this was part of his job description.

My mom and I quickly found out that one of the German girls in our group had met him before because she had been to this same hotel a couple of months before. They were both single, and Mom and I quickly started to create suspicious theories about what might have been a well-hidden, forbidden love story. It wasn't until the guide started listening to her more than to the whole group, that my mom and I launched some protest. And we won, of course. What was she thinking, deciding when to get on or off our horses? The Belgian girls got their way though!

Before we went on our first test ride, the owner of the stables, horses, and hotel – the tiny little Dutch woman – asked all of us specifically what kind of horse we liked. I asked her not to give me her easiest horse and she offered me the one who is normally in the front, ridden by the guide. Her name was Zoe and she was in every way different than the small, stubborn Thunderson I rode in France. Zoe was a chestnut mare – help! – and more of a leader type, a little more nervous, and very keen to canter in the areas where a canter was allowed. I noticed that Zoe did an amazing job climbing up and down the hills and mountains, galloping for minutes, and standing still whenever I asked her to. My mom, on the other hand, asked for a small horse because she does not like to ride big ones. She got the smallest one in the stables and boy, what a grumpy and mean little thing he was! As soon as you got on his back, he was fine but trying to get him cleaned and tacked up was a nightmare.

Well, it was a "night-gelding," more than a "nightmare." My mom was constantly talking to him as she was tacking him up and that would get me laughing, as she mostly just talked to herself. However, as soon as she got on his back, the night-gelding's worries and sorrows disappeared and he immediately went back to being a good boy.

The biggest part of our ride took us through the brown, rocky mountains of Crete. The only green color came from the countless olive tree plantations, that were always provided with a complex irrigation system of long black pipes above ground. These would sometimes be working while we were passing them, but the horses didn't even seem to notice them. I caught myself still feeling tense whenever we would pass something, I knew the previous thoroughbred I had ridden as a child would be scared of. I had been riding him for so many years that I knew him through and through and so I unwillingly projected his behavior and my preparedness for it on another horse.

The landscape was so brown and rocky because of the lack of rain on the island. Our guide told us this had worsened over the years because of global warming and in the meanwhile, I wondered whether these countless irrigation systems did any good to the water shortage. Besides the brown color, the presence of goats and sheep was overwhelming on the Cretan island. Everywhere we went, we would meet a flock of these animals and sometimes even their shepherd, who often looked like feral men who hadn't seen another human being in months, let alone a bath. This presence of sheep in the mountains brought along unwanted sightings of their bones as well; we would often pass along a white skeleton of an unfortunate sheep or goat, already bleached by the sun. One time we even spotted a huge griffon vulture, calmly resting alongside the road, watching the horses go by.

We passed through beautiful villages that looked like Heraklion but in a smaller and even older version. The houses were white to protect them from the sun's heat and some of them were painted blue. The streets were filled with children, their families sticking their head out of the window to marvel at the passing parade of horses. Sometimes, we would pass by a little Greek-Orthodox church, decorated with Greek flags. Whenever we were out in nature, we'd spot a lonely dilapidated house, probably owned by some shepherd who was herding a flock of sheep in the vicinity. What always struck me, was that every time we saw such a building, there would be a half-feral dog, chained to a pole and desperate to guard the house, but in the meantime longing for some attention or company to free him from his chains. It broke my heart to see these animals living in such poor conditions.

That third day, arriving at the Cretan coast, we learned we could go swimming with our horses. I must admit that it all started a little less heroic than I had imagined. After getting off our horses in this beautiful village on the Cretan coast, we unsaddled and gave them food and water. Then, the guide and another man – yes, a man, finally some reinforcements for the poor guide – drove us to our hotels. We quickly got into our bathing suits and returned to the horses, to get them to the shore and go into the water.

Have you ever seen a group of women in bathing suits, with their shoes on, leading a horse? Me neither. Judging by their faces, neither had all the men from the village. I suspect there are only certain dates where the tourists go into the sea with the horses and the villagers knew which days they were and marked them on their calendars. I wasn't sure what the men were staring at, I was dirty and red from the day's long ride in the mountains. I didn't look very fabulous. And no, my Vans shoes didn't make it better.

We arrived at the sea with our horses. My chestnut mare of course wouldn't get into the water at first. While everyone was gracefully splashing around in the seawater, I was still trying to pull Zoe further into the sea while my Vans sucked me to the bottom. I hadn't thought to bring any water shoes, of course. You'd think my mom would have thought about bringing this stuff in her months of preparation, but no.

Finally, our guide came to help me and I got on Zoe's back while we were in the water. This was the most amazing feeling in the world! Although I had thought nothing could be compared to my super-fast canter on the French coast, this was something completely different and somehow equally amazing. A couple of minutes later, I glanced at my mom and she looked a bit frightened. She yelled she was scared – even though she was on the smallest, but the meanest horse of the group. On top of all that, Zoe decided that enough was enough and she stopped moving altogether. Fortunately, the guide offered to trade horses and I had another nice swim with his young gelding who was still in training for trail riding. Back at the hotel, I had another laugh when my mom suddenly told me she thought this was a very cool experience and she wasn't afraid at all. It reminded me of when I would ask my boyfriend to kill a spider which he claims not to be afraid of but then refused to deliver... typical.

Our sea adventure taught me that even though I had been riding for so many years, there were still countless experiences to stumble across on horseback. This was one of the highlights of our trip and it is an experience I will never forget. It's a memory no one will ever be able to take away from my mom and I, which I will cherish for years to come.

I looked into my mother's eyes and a grin crossed my lips. Although our trip to Greece had come to an end, I couldn't help but ask her mischievously, "So, where shall we ride next?"

Pony Pals and Bush Mechanics

BY HEBE WEBBER

Whether it was coincidence or fate, I'll never know, but how all the horse crazy girls were put together in the same high school class was beyond me. Combined with the fact that most of us had our horses at the same agistment paddock which was walking distance from school, meant a recipe for absolute equine-related mischief. We soon ended up with nothing short of a real-life Saddle Club. And by Saddle Club I mean a low budget, Australian version of the series.

Sitting in the classroom, I glanced around at my friends. I could feel the afternoon suspense hanging in the air as we all stared at the clock, begging the seconds to tick by faster. Today was Wednesday, and that meant a golden ticket to half a day of freedom. We had lucked out in the best possible way, we were permitted to ride our horses for school sport.

Every Wednesday after lunch, when everyone else went to play soccer or tennis or some other form of what we considered to be boring, torturous school labor, we'd all walk together down to the paddock and go riding. We'd come up with the idea after sitting through such boredom longingly wishing we were on the backs of our horses. With much persuasion and the written permission of our parents, we had been granted our dream.

"RIINNNNGGGGGGG!!!" The abrupt sound of the bell snapped me out of my trance. Bolting for the door, I ignored the monotone comments of the teacher and grabbed my friend's arm. She turned around and grinned at me, saying "So... are we gonna take the horses to the lolly shop or the creek?"

Mischievously smiling back, I replied, "Why not both?" Meeting up with the other girls at the bus stop out front, we began the walk-through town and out to the horses.

During these afternoons we'd do all the things groups of young teenagers typically did but from the backs of our horses. It was not uncommon to see us riding along the foot-paths of town, across the main street, and park our horses outside the video store, while we went to the lolly shop or to buy hot chips and eat them in the park. The horses ate them with us too, of course. We found great joy in terrorizing the people walking through the parks by racing each other madly around and jumping over picnic benches, the only warning being a simple "watch out!" as we thundered by. Another favorite activity was racing the school bus, much to the horror of the driver and the delight of the kids, their faces pressed to the window as we waved to them from the back of our galloping steeds.

Hot and out of breath, we arrived at the paddock, sweat dripping down the backs of our shirts. As much as I hated it, I knew the heat meant the beginning of summer and summer meant long days with endless adventure opportunities. It may not have been the holidays yet, but today we were certainly in for an adventure.

Dumping my bag in the grass, I stepped up on the rickety, wooden gate, and screamed out my horse's name at the top of my lungs. "IIIIIINNNNNDDIIIIIIIIIII!!! CCC'MOOOOONNN!!!" Her head lifted, her big Arabian eyes observing me measuredly, calculating whether or not it was worth the effort to walk all the way over. "INDI!!" I belted out again. Yes, movement! She was on her way.

I hurried into the shed to grab a halter and organize my things for the ride. Shoving various rugs, girths, and saddle blankets out of the way in search of my own, I looked around the leaky, lean-to tin shed and sighed. It may not be much, but it was better than nothing. Australia is different to many countries, especially European countries, in that you do not have to be particularly wealthy to own a horse. There is so much land and so little people, that it is relatively cheap in comparison. Many agistment paddocks are not connected to riding schools or horse-related businesses, they are just fields owned by random people to whom you pay a small fee for the use of the land. This, and the complete lack of rules or adult supervision, were key elements in why we had so much fun.

Our agistment affectionately referred to as "The Paddock" was a simple field lined with trees, split in two. One side was owned by a car-obsessed, non-horsie guy who essentially let us do whatever we wanted without objection. He often assisted us in our mischief by giving us "paddock bombs" (old, unregistered cars) to drive around and various pieces of traffic control items to use as jumps or obstacle courses. The other side, which was owned by an older, hippie horse lady, had a tack room made from an old green rat-infested school bus with the seats ripped out. Generally, most things we had were makeshift. Jumps made from traffic cones, flowerpots, and old milk crates. Yards made of bamboo poles stuck together with baling twine. We used twine to make everything.

Finally finding my bridle amidst the chaos, I looked at it and groaned. The cheekpiece had been half-eaten by rats. Typical.

"Give me a look," my friend said snatching it off me as I walked outside. "It's fine, just bush mechanic it!"

Rolling my eyes, I turned around and went back into the shed in search of baling twine, Indi curiously staring at me from the gate to which she had arrived. "Bush mechanic-ing," or so we called it, was the art of fixing anything with baling twine. That is, the plastic twine used to bale hay. Saddles, rugs, bridles, girths, fences: you name it, we fixed it with twine. If being able to go out riding with your friends meant making a bridle out of the pieces of three different bridles and holding it together with twine, then you made it work. Today was one of those days.

"It's too hot for a helmet or pants," my friend exclaimed as she pulled herself onto her tall black horse. Shoes, helmets, and any form of tack were always optional during our escapades.

We looked a treat, me setting out bareback and barefoot in my newly bush mechanic-ed bridle, and her helmet-less in cut-off jeans, with bare feet sticking out of the metal stirrups.

"So, where to?" I mumbled to my friend, stopping my horse by a big, spiky plant on the side of the dirt road and stuffing my mouth full of wild bush raspberries. I think I already knew the answer.

"Hey guys, wait up!" A friend shouted to us, riding up the laneway that connected the two sides of the agistment, her chestnut pony spooking sideways as she yelled, another girl on a lanky white horse cantering closely behind her.

The four of us ate in silence for a moment, leaning forward to share the raspberries with our horses. "Let's go behind the houses," the girl on the white horse said, pushing her long dark hair out of her face. The youngest and most adventurous of us all, she had made a good choice. "Behind the houses" meant riding through the back suburb of the town, tearing up people's picture-perfect lawns, and just being a general neighborhood nuisance. Perfect for a Wednesday afternoon.

We rode up to the showground, stopping our prancing horses at the beginning of a short stretch of road that had houses on one side, and the local circus on the other. Leather creaked, hands tightened on reins. I could feel Indi bunching up beneath me, her eyes widening, ears flicking back and forth. She knew this was a spot we always cantered and was anticipating the race.

A whirlwind of white mane and thundering hooves suddenly went hurtling past. "Get outta the way!" My friend yelled, before turning around looking cheekily at us over the back of her cantering horse. "Race ya!" she said, already halfway down the lane. Taking off after her we flew down the lane to the chorus of barking dogs and yelling residents, trapeze artists staring in confusion out the back door of the circus as a bunch of laughing girls and galloping horses went flying past.

Winding in and out of pathways and interconnected streets, we let the horses catch their breath, giggling if they stopped to poo on people's lawns or leave muddy hoof prints across freshly mown grass. In a park alongside the river, at the back of all the houses, we stopped at a wide trunked tree.

"You're it!" I said tapping my friend on the shoulder, half shoving her off her black horse as I took off racing around the tree.

Bolting after me, she started madly yelling the rhyme, "Round and round the mulberry bush the monkey chased the weasel, the weasel thought it was fun and POP goes the weasel!" Horses weaving around each other and the tree, turning so tight they'd tuck up their haunches and almost spin on a dime. The game was that one person was "it" and would chase the rest of us around the tree, singing the rhyme. If the person caught you, you didn't just get a simple tap; most of the time you got "popped" off your horse—that is dragged off your galloping pony and onto the ground. We were fairly ruthless kids.

Bringing Indi to a halt, I turned around and heard the other girls scream excitedly as one was pulled off her horse and took another girl with her, both landing on the ground with a dull thud. Groaning and laughing, they clutched at their sides as they stood and dusted themselves off.

"Whadda you girls think you're doin!" A scowling man called over his back fence. Ignoring him and getting back on, we rode out of the park to a dirt motorbike track, using the jumps and banks as cross-country practice.

After haphazardly navigating the motorbike track, we appeared from the trees and stepped out into the streets. I raised my hand to my face to block the afternoon sun and scanned the houses. As we cruised along, I spotted what I was looking for. Stopping next to a passionfruit vine, I sneakily tried to squeeze Indi's fat body into the side of someone's front yard. Hurriedly snatching off the ripe fruit, I tossed some to my friends and another down my shirt. Out of the corner of my eye, I caught a movement in the house. I froze. "Sh*t!" caught red-handed. I looked around. "Horsie! Horsie! Hi, Horsie," a little girl waved to me from the window, her face pressed to the glass in delight.

Relieved, I back Indi out of the yard and heard the door open. The little girl was staring at me, eyes brimming with excitement. Clutching her shirt and bringing it up to her mouth, I knew the question she wanted to ask but was too afraid to let out. "Do you want to pat her?" I asked. The girl nodded and smiled, clambering down the stairs. Watching her stroke Indi's nose, I remembered being one of those little girls. I felt like I was helping to keep the horse girl dream alive through to the next generation.

Riding along the dusty home stretch of road belting out "The Saddle Club" theme song, we decided it was high time for a swim in the creek. After dumping our gear at the shed, we jumped bareback onto our sweaty horses and continued back down the road to the creek, riding in our bra and underwear like it was the normal, socially acceptable thing to do. I honestly never once considered this to be out of place.

Clutching Indi's mane as we trotted down the road, I was thankful to have my fat, round pinto pony. Riding her bareback was like sitting on a big squishy sofa. A big squishy sofa with a big attitude. Half Arabian, half unknown pinto pony mongrel, Indiana was the kind of bomb-proof, yet crazy pony all kids come to both love and loathe. She was completely unflappable on the ground yet turned into a bolting nightmare at any hill or a long stretch of grass. She certainly taught me how to stay on. Despite her bad habits, she was my best friend and longtime companion that I could never part with.

Crashing through the undergrowth down the trail to the creek, I swatted flies, hanging caterpillars, spiderwebs, and various other insects out of our way. It always paid not to be first, better to have the path cleared by someone else. But Indi was the best bush horse of them all, so first she went. She may not have been a fancy, pushbutton pony that worked in a frame and won

ribbons at the show, but that horse went anywhere. No hill was too steep or bush too thick.
Always bloody going first! I thought to myself as
I precariously removed a spiky, wait-a-while
bush from my leg, spots of blood beginning to
bead on my thigh. These thin green vines are
hard to spot in the jungle undergrowth and have
sets of spines along their sides. These spines
stick into your skin or clothes, and take forever
to pull off, hence the name "wait a while."

Walking down into the creek, all the other
girls piling in behind me, our horses took a long
drink then pawed and rolled and splashed, letting out big sighs of satisfaction. They loved the
adventures going to the creek. Half the time we
didn't have to hold them, they'd just stay there
while we went for a swim. Without tack, free to
come and go as they pleased, usually choosing to
happily nap in the shallows or take themselves in
for a swim.

As Indi waded deeper into the water, I felt
her hooves lift off the bottom, and her body sink
as she started to swim. Slipping off her side, I
grabbed onto her mane as she towed us both
along. As the cool water rushed over us both, I
thought about her nickname "Hippo Pony" and
smiled to myself. She got it because, well, she
was notoriously overweight and two because she
would guard the waterhole like an angry Mumma
hippo, putting her ears back and threatening any
horse that tried to swim while she was in there.
Right now nothing suited her more as she
bobbed along in the water, lips pulled up over

her teeth so she had this big, goofy grin that looked like something out of a cartoon.

"Oi guys, check this out!" My friend called. Sliding back on as I felt Indi's hooves make contact with the hard ground again, I turned around to see my friend's blonde hair disappear into the murky water, as she took a deep breath and swam beneath her pony's belly. The chestnut mare's eyes bulged, ears flicking back, but she didn't move a muscle. Popping up out of the water on the other side, my friend grinned, sodden leaves sticking to her face. "Anyone else?" she dared, the trickster among us.

"I've got a better idea," I retorted before anyone could try and make me swim under my pony. After much shuffling, a few flattened ears, and a couple of attempted kicks I got them all to line their horses up next to mine, heads to the bank, and rumps to the water. "Ok, so the one who can make the biggest bomb into the water wins, alright?" Everyone nodded in agreement. Leaving our reins hanging around their necks, we all stood on their rumps and jumped off "bombing" into the water. Resurfacing amidst the splashing and jumping, I could see the horses still patiently standing in a line. If you want to literally "bomb proof" a horse, give it to a bunch of kids... Trust me.

Reaching to grab Indi's reins, she swerved slightly away from me in the water. "Aww Indi c'mon, don't be like that!" I said to her. Evidently, she'd had enough of our antics, and starting striding out of the water towards the trail home. "No, no, no... INDI!" I yelled, wincing as my bare feet slipped over rocks hidden beneath the murky water. Tripping up onto the bank, I went to chase after her, but it was too late. With a toss of her head, she took off down the trail. Damn. I stood there dripping wet, hands-on-hips, watching as she disappeared from view. The other girls were in stitches, crying with laughter at my predicament. It was a regular occurrence to see a fat pinto pony running down the street, closely followed by an out of breath girl yelling "Indiiiiii!" I didn't find it quite so funny, though to them I think it got funnier every time.

"Come on, let's go get her," my friend on the black horse said, grabbing my hand and using her barefoot to boost me up behind her. Slipping around on her horse's wet back, I clasped my hands around her stomach and leaned my head against her shoulder. She was always acting like the big sister in the group, knowing when to push us to our limits or to give us a helping hand. I appreciated her presence so much, especially right now.

"Thanks," I said, smiling up at her.

"No problem," she smiled back kindly, guiding her horse over the twisted roots on the embankment. Doubling bareback down to the paddock, we found Indi exactly where I thought she'd be: contentedly eating grass out the front of the gate as if nothing had ever happened. Seeing us, she walked smugly over to the hitching rail and parked herself in the usual spot.

I jumped down off my friend's horse and grabbed her reins. Indi knew she was in trouble but didn't seem to care. "How could you!" I hissed at her. She snorted back in my face. "Thanks a lot, Indi," I grumbled, removing her bridle. Yawning, Indi started rubbing her wet, sweaty head up and down my back, pushing me with her nose, before letting her head come to rest on my chest. "Hey! Stop it!" I giggled, not really meaning it. She then stood eyes shut, unmoving except for the quivering of her lips, letting out a deep sigh. I knew this behavior was rude, invading my personal space, but still, my heart melted. How could I be mad with a pony so special? Cradling her head in my arms, I stared down at her. Surely it was something extraordinary when a horse surrenders itself to you, in complete vulnerability? I hoped so. I was proud to hold her the way she so often held me.

"Guess what tomorrow is?" My friend said to me as I stepped through the fence and into the yard.

"What is it?" I replied with a distrusting look, unsure whether or not I wanted to know.

"Tomorrow is the first weekend of the summer holidays." She sat on the steps of the old green rusted school bus, popping pony pellets into her mouth. "And that means we're camping out!" I sat down next to her. It was steadily getting dark and we were waiting for our lifts home, sheltering in the rat-infested old bus. The inside had the seats ripped out and served as the tack room on this side of the agistment.

"And it also means, the sugarcane fields are waiting for us," I said leaning back against the moldy sideboard lining the stairs. I eyed the pony pellets. I was absolutely starving. But from experience, I'd learned that most horse feed doesn't always taste as good as it smells. Maybe that was due to the rats. I grimaced. Ignoring the thought, I popped a few in my mouth. Tentatively crunching them, I was happily surprised. Pony pellets weren't so bad, they tasted kind of like Weetbix—a breakfast cereal biscuit manufactured in Australia.

"Good, hey?" My friend exclaimed.

"Yeah... give me some more," I said, reaching for another handful. Laughing I said, "We'd better remember to bring some more snacks when we go camping!"

Summer campouts were what we spent all year waiting for. We'd ride sun up till sundown, pitching a tent in the middle of the paddock but half the time end up sleeping under the stars wrapped in our horse rugs. Staring up at the stars and giggling to one another, the horses would graze curiously around us, poking their noses into sleeping bags to try and find treats. If we didn't camp, we stayed at the hippie horse lady's house on the hill. Sometimes her horses would come inside the house and help themselves to the fruit bowl, so it was no surprise when you'd turn around and see a tail disappearing out the door.

We'd stay up late watching old horse movies and listening to her stories. We'd hang off every word, imaginations running wild as we sipped on hot tea gazing up at her face, every moment animated by the candlelight that surrounded us. She had a big double sliding glass window along one wall, big enough that up to three horses could stand together with their chests pressed against it and their entire necks and heads inside the lounge room. I remember so vividly one morning, sitting there in the open frame of the window. Still in my pajamas, legs hanging out over the edge, sharing a bowl of porridge with my pony through the window as we planned the day's adventures.

Summer on the subtropical east coast of Australia also meant rainy season. I could feel the thick, sticky humid summer air clinging to my skin. Maybe it was from camping outside and in Indi's rug last night. Waking with the sun, we had headed out to our friend's farm where we were about to begin one of our favorite summer games: racing in the wet sugarcane fields.

Sugarcane is grown in long aisles, separated by long flat stretches of grass with deep irrigation ditches dug alongside. Big enough for both you and your horse to fall in, if you were unlucky. Heart pounding, eyes glued to the end of the field, I waited for the call. We were all lined up at the end of each aisle, horses prancing in anticipation. Flashing cheeky grins at each other, we gathered up our reins. The call began "One.... Two... Three..." At that moment before the word "go," time seemed to stand still. No sound. Everything froze. It was as if the world was holding its breath. The only thing that remained was the pounding of your heart and the sound of your horse's breath. Eyes on the horizon, then the final call: "GO!"

Horse's back legs surging beneath them, zero to a hundred in one second flat. Flying down the aisle, mud spraying in all directions, all I could see of my friends next to me were their helmets flashing through the top of the sugarcane, horse's invisible beneath them.

Tears streamed down my face from the force of the wind rushing past. I was covered in mud but I didn't care. I loved the feeling of Indi giving it all she's got, the pure raw power of her stride beneath me. I crouched lower over her neck and urged her faster, everything around us a blur. "Ya, ya c'mon Indi!" Ears flattened, she powered forward like a bullet from a gun.

Whooping and cheering, we all came sliding to a stop through the mud at the end of the aisles, arguing over who came first. The fun wasn't really in the winning or losing, it was in the chase itself.

As summer rolled out and winter rolled in, the pony club season would kick in. Luckily for us, the showground where the club days were held was only a five-minute ride up the road. None of us could afford horse trailers, so it was even luckier that we knew a local Standardbred trainer with a big six-horse truck that would take us to any gymkhana we wanted for a small fee. Going to the pony club added a sense of purpose to our riding and adventures. We had something to aim for, to work towards. Of course, just as our gear was, our pony club was fairly makeshift and low budget.

It was an interesting rivalry, in that we shared our club grounds with another pony club. The other club was full of the more privileged type kids who only rode because their parents forced it upon them, not because they wanted to. Most of us kids considered ourselves incredibly lucky to even have the chance to ride a horse, and you wouldn't dare tell a soul if the horse was naughty or dangerous for fear it might be taken away from you. Better to have a psychopathic pony than no pony at all.

Walking Indi across the competition grounds, I heard a sneer and a giggle. Looking around, I could see the kids from the club we shared our grounds by pointing at us. Glaring at them I marched forward, determined not to let their attitudes ruin my day. I stood out like a sore thumb, not just because I was wearing the tell-tale purple and green colors of my club, but because I had a fat hairy pinto pony with a long mane and tail, and rode in a dressage saddle for every discipline. All of the previous attributes are a big "NO" in the pony club scene. It's asking to be picked on. Even though most of the kids in my club didn't have fancy gear, and not always the stereotypical "nice" horse, I swear we had so much more fun.

"All gear and no idea they are," I said to Indi, referring to the sniggering kids. "Never mind them." After the morning's miseries over hacking, in which true to my club's reputation, I placed 6th in a group of six riders, I was ready to tear it up in sporting (in Australia we refer to mounted games as "sporting"). This was when the real fun was had. Everyone took off their club jumpers and ties, pulled out their horse's plaits, and put on their club jerseys. Everything was about to get a little less serious, and a whole lot more exciting.

Lining up along the fence, the atmosphere was electric. Over the top of the loudspeaker announcements, we screamed encouragement at each other from the sidelines, even if our horses behaved badly. This was our time when all the crazy backstreet adventures on bush ponies felt like they amounted to something in the horse world.

After flying around barrels, pole bending, and flags we were ready as anything for the relay race. This meant we competed together as a team, rather than individually. It was a great way to finish up the weekend by sharing something together. Because we were all great friends and always rode together, these kinds of races came to us like second nature. Prepping Indi at the start line, my friend galloped towards me. At the exact moment she pushed a small metal pole into my hand, Indi took off like a lightning bolt. Just managing to keep it in my hand, we raced against the clock. Darting over the jump and twisting around the pole at the end of the line, we were in best bet for first place. Grasping the metal relay pole tighter, I felt the smooth, cool metal press into my hand as we ran down the final stretch. It was one of those moments again, just like in the cane fields. Time stood still, the shouts of my teammates faded. Thundering hooves and a pounding heart filled my mind. This is why we rode, this is what we lived for. To share these moments with our horses and our friends, a celebration of connection, teamwork, pure joy, and absolute fun. Pressing the relay pole into the next girl's hand, I caught a glimpse of her face. My friend had that same look, determined eyes set the course ahead. I knew she was about to experience what I just had. And better yet, she'd take our team across the finish line in first place.

High-fiving my friends as I rode an over-excited, sweaty Indi into the line of horses, I was stoked. I loved my horse. I loved my friends. We were all so lucky to have each other. While all the other kids with expensive ponies and gear would sulk around, we were constantly laughing. We flew around having the time of our lives, our horses not blinking an eye while their "push-button ponies" spooked at the obstacle courses. I could have sworn sometimes the indignant glares and hurtful comments from those kids were actually out of jealousy rather than pity. It was us that pitied them when we saw how little they enjoyed what we loved. It seemed that the less stuff you had, the less you had to worry about. I'd take our club's friendship and camaraderie over expensive horses and gear any day.

Now, to take you back to how this all began, let's just say that all of these Saddle Club adventures were made possible by a small amount of luck, a little bit of chance, and almost entirely out of divine timing.

Eleven-year-old me was bored and frustrated with structured riding lessons. As all kids do, I wanted fun and freedom, not someone yelling at me while I cantered in a circle for the hundredth time. But since owning a pony was not an option,

I set about putting handwritten signs up at local corner stores. The sign said I was an "experienced" eleven-year-old that could ride or look after your horse for $10 an hour. I think the ad even featured some glittery horse stickers. Cute, I know. Every afternoon I'd stop by the store to see if someone had ripped off one of the contact numbers. After a while, a couple went missing, though I'm sure it was Dad taking them just to keep my hopes up. But as the weeks rolled by, no one answered. Disheartened, I began to think that my dream may not become a reality. Until one day, it did.

"I need to talk to you about something..." Dad said as we walked over to the table. "Somebody answered your ad." I sat down, staring back at him wide-eyed in anticipation.

"Really?!" My reply came out as a half squeal, half-whisper.

"Yes," he said, looking me in the eye. "They have a pony they want you to look after." I couldn't believe it. Fifteen years later I still remember this moment like it was yesterday. I was lucky that from that day forth, I borrowed Indi for a total of five years before I owned her. By some strange coincidence, Indi and I were the same age. We were with each other from age eleven until 22. And to be honest, I don't even really like to use the word owner... it doesn't sit right. The intonation of "owner" gives some sense that one has more power over the other, one of us makes the rules. Indi was my friend, my sister, my equal. And she definitely made the rules!

It is a special kind of bond when you go through adolescence alongside a horse. Throughout all the emotional and physical changes, they are a constant true friend, free of judgment and ridicule. The fearlessness and sense of invincibility you have as a teenager, coupled with the power and freedom of a horse, taught me the true meaning of the saying, "Thou shalt fly without wings and conquer without any sword." They become an extension of yourself, a centaur connection. Indi was my equine twin flame.

I remember evenings cantering along the road, bareback in a halter, staring up at the stars, and breathing in the balmy summer night air. Closing my eyes and raising my hands to the sky. Feeling her warm coat against my legs, listening to the sound of her breath and the steady thudding of her hooves as she carried us home. Such pure trust I've never known since. Sometimes I would take a nap in the field with her, the sounds of her munching grass like a meditation. More often than not she would come and watch over me while I dozed, her front hooves pressed in close and letting her head drop down near mine, in the same way a mare protects her sleeping foal. If I didn't take a nap on the ground, I would take a nap on her back, my bare feet hooked over her withers, and my head resting on her rump. It was like this my parents found me one winter night when they were late to pick me up.

Thinking that they'd forgotten me in the dark and cold, I'd fallen asleep on Indi's back beneath her winter rug, with just my head poking out on her rump. I'm not sure my parents saw the situation in the same safe and comfortable way that I did. But when I look back, I see Indi as my fat, hairy, grass munching guardian angel. She tolerated my "training" sessions, which essentially involved eleven-year-old me trying to bomb-proof an already bomb proofed pony by chasing her around with plastic bags tied onto sticks and bouncing bright pink oversize exercise balls on her back. I also thought it was great fun to run up to her while she was rolling and jump on her back just as she was about to get up. She would then lift me with her as she stood up. I dubbed this game "camel pony," because it felt like you were riding a camel.

The things kids do.

Although I was blessed with a pony who was quiet to handle in every way, I was not so blessed when it came to riding. She was a fireball disguised in an innocent hairy fat suit. That pony could go, and when she went there was no stopping her. You generally had two options: Abort mission or cling on for dear life and pray for mercy. She would gallop uncontrollably faster and faster towards a jump or until she reached a fence, and either stop dead at the last second or swerve abruptly to the side. This generally resulted in you going over the jump without her. Most trail rides were spent going sideways, as she pranced and frothed with sweat. If she didn't do that, she did the exact opposite: stop and go backward. No amount of encouragement got her to go forward again, she would simply go back faster. Even with her behavioral issues, I loved her all the same. It gave her character. I loved her intelligence, her expressive face, and big Arabian eyes. My friendship with Indi was something so precious and unique, I know I'll never meet another horse who was quite like her.

Having Indi by my side and my group of horsie friends as an adolescent was a blessing, I am forever grateful for. Interestingly enough, save one or two, most of us weren't friends outside of the horse scene. In those golden years, we were glued to our horses, which in turn glued us all together.

As the years went by, things began to change. We grew older and some of us moved on to bigger horses, selling our first ones or mourned the loss of our dearest companions. We left school, some of us moved away. The field where we once rode is now a housing estate. But fifteen years on, most of us still ride. Though we don't all keep in contact, when we do see each other we can't help but reminisce on those golden years.

The majority of the horses are gone now, but I think of them every day. Whenever I see the ones that are still here, I smile at their greying faces and stroke their swaying backs, though it puts a lump in my throat. They gave us so much. There are not enough words in the world to tell them how grateful I am. Our friendships and adventures together shaped who we are today. Without adults, rules, or help we learned to be self-reliant, have courage and confidence in our abilities, and be adaptable to any situation that we may find ourselves in. This resilience helped me to travel the world alone and instilled in me a thirst for adventure. This thirst took me to ride horses across the globe, from living with Chilean Gauchos to riding through Guatemala with gypsies.

I can distinctly remember being on a riding holiday in Croatia, and my reins snapping mid-gallop. Many of the other riders were deeply concerned, thinking I'd have to walk my horse back home. The guide offered me his bridle, but I refused. Unconcerned, I pulled off the broken part of my reins and tied them back together in true bush mechanic fashion. The guide then looked me in the eye with a knowing smile, saying in his thick Croatian accent, "You have done this before. You are a very smart girl."

I may not be riding on million-dollar horses and aiming for the Olympics, but I am proud of where I've come from. I am so incredibly lucky to have had the adolescence that I did, it is an opportunity not so many get to have. It may have been on a borrowed pony, in a broken bridle, and using the same dressage saddle for every discipline but all these things are what made it possible. Seeing us all grow and change into where we are today and remembering the one constant that brought us here: the friendship of our horses and each other. So here's to the friendships that we've had before, the ones we still have, and the adventures yet to come.

Strangers in Ireland: A 400 Mile Journey

BY KRYSTAL KELLY

I hesitated as my fist hovered above the door. I took in a deep breath, bracing myself for whatever—and whoever—may be standing behind the closed door. After all, it was a complete stranger's house. And I wasn't exactly invited...

Knock, Knock, Knock!

I gently tapped on the door, my nerves defeated by the very real concern for my two horses. They were counting on me and whether I liked it or not, I had been the one who had gotten us into this situation.

I turned for a quick glance behind me, just to be sure my horses were ok in my absence. My husband stood patiently in the drive, holding their reins. At this point we had been on the road for nearly a month and a half... their ears pointed forward all too knowingly as they patiently stood waiting for the "Ok" signal. They knew the drill.

The door creaked open and revealed a disheveled looking man. He appeared to have been in the middle of cooking dinner, the smell of a hot meal wafted from the kitchen. I forced a smile as my rumbling stomach beckoned.

"Hi," I began, "My name is Krystal. I'm from California and my husband is from Germany." I pointed behind me towards the curious group of watchful eyes. I continued quickly, praying he wouldn't slam the door shut in my face before I finished everything I had to say. "We are riding our two horses across Ireland and we need a field for them to sleep tonight. Do you have a spare field for them for the night and maybe a place where we could pitch our tent?"

The man paused. My heart pounded.

This had been the fourth door we had knocked on this evening and the daylight was already beginning to fade. I silently knew that this man's answer would determine whether or not my band of companions would be risking walking in the dark as we continued to knock on doors.

"I don't know if I should be doing this, because of insurance and all... but if you promise not to sue me then I have a spare field for your horses. But I don't know if I should be doing this!" The man stepped outside his house, motioning for us to follow him. "The field is this way. I also happen to have an abandoned house which is in the process of being refurbished. It's not much, and I don't know if I should be doing this," he continued as our horses stepped in unison with us. "But it has a working fireplace while I'm drying the fresh paint and it will get you out of the freezing cold tonight."

"Thank you, thank you!" I struggled to keep up with him as he led us to the field. Lilly, my part-Arabian mare, however had no trouble keeping up with him. She strolled past me, knowing that there was a new field awaiting her, ready for her to enjoy a good roll followed by her daily investigating of the new surroundings. She always felt right at home no matter where we seemed to end up.

My lips pursed as my eyes looked upwards towards the sky. I let out a silent laugh. *How the hell did I get myself into this?*

60 Days Earlier.

I had just finished all of my pre-planned travels for the year. I had been hired by multiple stables for my equestrian travel documentary series for our YouTube Channel on Equestrian Adventuresses. Being on the road felt natural to me. Its a lifestyle I had chosen for myself nearly a decade ago when I left California for good.

My husband, Christian, on the other hand, wasn't as homesick for the road as I had been the past two years. Sure, we had enjoyed an exciting life as newlyweds in England, a country we were both unfamiliar with. And yes, I had occasionally taken solo trips to exotic countries for quick getaways to suppress my thirst for adventure... but somehow it hadn't fully satiated that hunger.

My eyes scanned my laptop as I searched for an alternative. After all, Christian had long since left his comfortable "office-job" as an engineer.

We had moved out of our apartment and currently had all of our belongings in storage in Germany. And we were the proud owners of two lovely horses, whom we'd trained for the past two years who were energetic and ready for exploring.

Why not have a grand adventure as a family? It was now or never.

My email inbox had an unread message. I hovered to open it.

"Dear Krystal," the message read. "I found your website when I was looking for Women's Travel Safety courses and was delighted to see the work you do with horses! I live in Ireland and I would love to know if you are planning on coming to Ireland sometime. We could use a great coach like you because around where I live there are limited options. Do let me know if you ever plan to come this way. Sincerely, Ciara."

I sat up in my chair, excited. I had been silently toying with the idea of riding my horses in the country of my family heritage. It would be silly to say that as a horse-crazy adolescent, I hadn't dreamed of being like one of the boys from the film, "Into the West," riding a horse across the countryside of Ireland.

I began typing furiously, "Thank you for reaching out to me! I actually have not been to Ireland yet BUT funny you should mention..."

And so our adventure began.

40 Days Before Departure.

Before my husband and horses had time to blink, we were waiting for a horse-box transport to come and pick us up. We had spent the past month couch surfing at a friend of ours with endurance horses. I knew them from working as a riding coach and trainer for the yard off and on and had grown quite close with the owner of the stables. Her beautiful home was the epitome of my "British fantasy," mixed with a hint of the American West. Her love of the cowboy life and the western decor, coated with a British accent made me feel right at home.

We had thoroughly enjoyed our stay with our friends. It had been a humbling experience as they adorned our horses with makeshift sheepskin saddle pads for our horse, Q, a 16.1hh ex-racing thoroughbred mare with thin skin and a bossy nature. Even I had been upgraded with a new down jacket. "Take this, you'll never survive the rain and cold in that jacket," they stuffed the coat in my hands.

"I've heard it might rain in Ireland..." I laughed.

The morning of the horsebox's arrival was a hectic one. I had one final loose end to tie before departing on our big journey... my car. But not just any car. It was my hot pink rally car, a 2000 Toyota Yaris junky rust-bucket of a machine. The very car that three years earlier I had bought randomly on eBay for $700 and drove halfway around the world to Mongolia and back again.

But it wasn't just the car that gave me the road trip of a lifetime. It was the very reason my husband and I had met. We met whilst awaiting a ferry boat in Azerbaijan to take my car and myself across the Caspian Sea into Turkmenistan.

I drove my car to the nearest dealership, whose promise to "buy any car" was a motto I was counting on. After all, if this didn't work, I would be in trouble. Christian had left with our two horses before I did. They were both saddled. He rode his mare Q proudly, ponying Lilly beside him as he disappeared into the forest. "See you in an hour!" He called in the distance.

I dropped off my car, gave her a final pat on the hood for good-bye, and stuffed the 50 quid into my pocket. Then I wore my helmet, confusing the onlookers, and strolled down the street to meet my official "only-means-of-transportation," Lilly.

We arrived back in the stables just as the horsebox pulled into the yard. We loaded up, said our goodbyes and jumped in the front seat. The driver and owner of the horsebox was familiar with the crossing over to Ireland.

"A lot of racehorses come to England to run," he explained. We had a long drive ahead of us, including one ferry crossing from midnight to around 4am. Then it was another three hours to Ciara's.

"So, do you know where you're going to stay the day after tomorrow?" He asked, pondering our big ride from the South to the North of Ireland.

"Not a clue," I grinned. And all was right with the world again.

The Day of Departure.

Ciara had become a good friend from the moment we met. It was almost as if we had already known one another and hadn't been strangers a few weeks ago. Our horses had settled in beautifully, enjoying their view of the ocean and strange 'mooing creatures' in the distance. We were nestled in County Cork, a place that to this day remains in my heart as one of the most scenic places on Earth.

Christian and I had been preparing our horses with the saddlebags only briefly and were secretly nervous as to how they would handle the weight of the equipment. Though we packed extremely light, we had foolishly purchased a tent which was a tad too large, hoping that the bonus porch section would come in handy to keep our saddles and equipment dry in what we assumed to be a future two months of rain.

We saddled our horses, spending a good three hours fumbling with all the bags and equipment, trying our best to make it stay in place without rubbing our poor horse's coats.

I've been working with horses for 15 years as a professional coach and trainer at many top stables with Olympic horses... and yet here I was a total amateur, fighting with my rain poncho as I desperately tried to bungee it in place.

Our horses, though not quite experts at carrying saddlebags, were however, familiar with endurance rides and adventures. At home in England we spent six days a week at the stables, even with Christian's full-time job, riding and training our horses. We played polo with them, entered them in low level jumping and dressage competitions, Christian practiced his groundwork and horsemanship skills and once a month we loaded them up and took them on different endurance rides as a way of seeing the beautiful countryside.

It was those endurance rides that had convinced Christian that he needed to live his childhood fantasy of being a cowboy and riding his horse across the prairie. Funny coming from an engineer who specialized in motorcycles, cars and all things engines.

Christian absolutely adored Q, or Q Twenty Girl as she had been known on the track. She was the slowest racehorse that lived (probably), coming in dead-last in nearly every race. When we first moved to England, I had bought us Lilly, a spunky part-Arabian mare with little training and a great attitude. Lilly had been the first horse Christian had ever encountered as an adult and he took his training with me seriously, taking riding lessons every other day alternating the lessons with groundwork sessions. After a year of dressage shows and an all intensive all-things-horsey bootcamp with me, it was time for him to get a horse of his own.

I found Q for him because she was tall and more suited to his tall and lean build. Not to mention she was dead quiet, but fast enough for him to enjoy his all-time favorite thing... galloping.

And yet here we were committed to a two-month trip across a country carrying saddlebags and riding on roads. We would be riding our horses and walking on foot when necessary, but one thing was certain, there would be no fast paces on this trip. That's right. We owned two beautiful Ferrari's and were using them for city driving for the foreseeable future.

Nevertheless, this was an experience that would be sure to bond our little herd together in a way no other form of training could accomplish...

"That's it!" I shouted triumphantly, "All finished! We are ready to go." I gave Lilly a little pat on her neck, thanking her for being so patient with me. Her eyes were bright, as usual, ready to tackle whatever obstacle I put in front of her. Q was enjoying a little snooze in the sunshine. Her resting foot and drooping lower lip showed absolutely no signs of distress over the packs and tent strapped to the back of her saddle.

"This is so exciting," Ciara shrieked. "Let's take a commemorative photo!"

I couldn't believe how lucky we were to have found Ciara. To think we had been staying at her beautiful home for several days now, all because of a random email in my inbox.

"I'll start driving around 2pm and meet you at Sharon's house! Good luck and enjoy your ride!" She gave us each a hug, horses included. She held onto their reins as we each failed miserably at swinging our legs over the bulk of the packs as we tried to mount.

"That's going to take some getting used to..." I groaned, feeling like a total idiot for the fifteenth time that morning. At least there was one thing I was certain about... Lilly and Q were professionals.

Day Three.

"Are you looking for the O'Conner's farm?" A strange man had pulled his pickup truck over, calling to us from his rolled down window.

"Yeah!" I smiled. I guess not too many horse riders carrying everything they owned in their backpacks and saddlebags would have been riding down this particularly quiet country lane.

"You're going the right way," he smiled. "Keep following this road and when it comes to an end you head right and then take the second left. That will take you all the way there."

"Thank you!"

"Beautiful horses," he waved as he drove off. I smiled proudly, patting my lovely mare on her neck. She didn't care much for stopping, she was on a mission and had until sundown to accomplish the job. I laughed and dropped the reins, holding only the buckle on the very end as she power walked forward. She seemed to know where she was going and it wouldn't surprise me if she understood the man's directions.

We arrived a good two hours before sunset. It was September and so far the weather had been surprisingly sunny and on our side. We had lucked out for the third day in a row. A friend of a friend of a friend had referred us to our current destination, a quaint dairy farm located exactly en-route to our first big riding goal: the Mizen Head Peninsula.

"Hello," I hopped off Lilly as the family residing at the dairy farm stepped out of their home to greet us. I wasn't sure if it was the sound of the horse's hooves that gave away our arrival, the friendly man in the car warning them we were near, or if they had been watching us from the window for the past half hour as we climbed up the road, past their cows. Their house was situated with quite an impressive view, the sea sparkling not too far in the distance.

"I'm Krystal, that's Christian and Q, and this is Lilly. Nice to meet you." I shook the woman's hand, followed by her teenage daughter. They led us to the field where our horses would be staying for the night.

"We cleared all the cows out of the field this morning so the horses have it all to themselves!" The woman, Roisin, gave Lilly a loving pat. "You can put your saddles and things here and cover it with the tarp here so it can stay dry tonight. And when you're ready come inside, I have dinner cooking!"

Christian and I looked to each other, smiling. Admittedly we had only been on the road for three days now, and only in Ireland for about one week, but in that time we had yet to use our tent or suffer without a hot meal.

Hallelujah.

We staggered into the house after sorting our horses and gear and were welcomed with the smell of food in the oven. A man by the name of Kevin greeted us at the door. "C'mon in, don't be shy," he had a big smile stretched across his face. I started to wonder if there was something in the water that made nearly everyone in this country so dang friendly.

They showed us to our room—that's right we had an actual bed...again! —and then sat with us at the dinner table. Kevin, Roisin and their daughter, Emily, inquired about our adventure as we ate. The conversation steered towards their family life as dairy farmers and soon Christian found himself volunteering to help milk the cows that evening.

After finishing his chores helping out with the hundred cows that needed daily milking, Kevin invited the both of us to his favorite pub. We couldn't say no to an offer like that so he drove us to the Mizen head, the most southernly point in Ireland and our destination the next day. It just so happened that the Mizen head also hosted the most southernly bar in Ireland, a place which had also hosted several awards and photos for having been featured in films.

We enjoyed the night out getting to know the culture. We talked for hours, really getting a sense for not only the journey we were up against riding across a country with paved roads and speedy drivers, but also a sense for the customs, the life, the history and more.

We slept easily that night. Not only had this family turned out to be extremely kind and generous to allow us into their home, they also offered us a promising stay the next two nights as we rode to the Mizen Head. They owned a Bed and Breakfast with a small field which in the summer months is used as a camper van and spot for tourists to pitch their tents.

Luckily, having started our ride so late in the year, all the tourists had vacated and we enjoyed a spectacular view along the coast on quiet back roads. We covered about 30 kilometers that day and when we arrived at their BnB we were stunned speechless. The BnB where we would be sleeping was gorgeous, and Roisin had driven there sometime during our ride and stocked the kitchen with fruits and toast and the makings for an Irish breakfast as well as a frozen pizza for dinner.

The horses had an equally amazing home for the next two nights while we rested and explored the nearby beaches. The field came right up to the house and for the first time the horses had a view of the waves crashing against the rocks. The waves were rough and the horses, even after 30 kilometers and about a 5-hour ride, trotted around the field with their tails in the air as they eyeballed the sea.

"If this is the start of our trip," Christian turned to me, equally impressed by the view and our good fortunes, "then I can't even imagine what is yet to come..."

Two Weeks In.

Our luck had somehow carried us to yet another friendly host that evening. Christian and I pulled into the stables, eager for the day's long ride to be done. We were greeted and shown two empty stalls with fresh bedding.

"You can unsaddle your horses here and then I'll show you to the field where they can stay tonight," Chris, our host for the night, said. He headed off down the stables to finish his other tasks.

We had been referred to this stable from a Facebook post. I had been sharing our journey on my Facebook page and I found that the news of our travels spread like wildfire across the equestrian community. We had countless messages in our inbox of people offering us a place for the night for ourselves and our horses. We tried to take note of the places in route as best as we could. We had yet to knock on a total stranger's door asking for a field and place to pitch our tent, as had been the plan, but that was about to change.

Today was the last stop we had sourced ahead of time along the way and a dark cloud hung over us as we knew when we woke the next morning we would be riding into uncertainty. I tried my best not to think about the scary, gut-wrenching idea that tomorrow we may or may not find a place for our horses to sleep for the night.

But tomorrow was still a long way away and I stuffed the fear deep inside and instead focused on our evening plans. Chris returned and we led our horses to their field for the night. All the other horses whinnied at the pretty bay mares as they walked by. Once loose, Lilly began her evening field inspections whereas Q enjoyed a good roll.

We were invited in the house for dinner, another hot meal! I sat at the table feeling a bit like a fraud. Here I was a "hard core" adventurer and yet I had yet to spend a night in our tent or bust out the cooker we had brought with us for a ramen noodle dinner.

Chris's son, Lucas appeared and we all began talking horses. Before we knew it Christian and I were swept back inside the stables to try our hand at something we hadn't expected.

"Meet Tiny!" Lucas appeared, miniature pony in hand.

Christian had shared his dream of learning to drive a carriage as well as his other dream to try his hand at stunt riding...and well, here we were, about to have his dreams come true.

They tacked Tiny up and led him to the indoor arena. Lucas showed Christian how to attach the Sulky (cart) to him. Tiny was a stallion that knew his job and soon Tiny and Christian were trotting around the arena, zig zagging around the obstacle course of cones which Lucas had diligently placed around the arena. Christian couldn't stop laughing.

But that wasn't all. Next, after Tiny had been put away and enjoyed a good roll for a good day's work, they brought out the big guns. The thunder of hooves echoed through the stables as Chris led the large draft mare into the arena. She was adorned with a thick pad on her back and a surcingle for vaulting. Christian was instructed how to mount from the ground, which he succeeded after only three attempts—damn his athleticism—and then was sent round the circle on a lunge while Chris gave him a variety of tasks to perform.

The amount of laughter that took place that evening was a good reminder of why we were doing what we were doing. To have fun with horses. Because really, is there any better reason than that?

Three Weeks In.

Tonight, was not the night. Why, of all the nights, did it have to be tonight, the night before an approaching hurricane, that we couldn't find a place to stay?!

Typical.

We had asked everyone. The men with horses and jaunting carts taking tourists around the national park. The hotel receptionists. We had knocked on every house in sight, several of which appeared to have had an empty field attached to their yard, though they claimed to not know of any fields before closing the door on our homeless and weary faces.

I had even tried calling the national park rangers. The only outcome of the frenzy was a small piece of grass beside the busy road which, according to the park ranger and jaunting cart drivers claimed to be "common land." There was no fence and only a single tree to tie our horses. We had unsaddled them right there on the roadside as they tangled themselves in their long ropes, completely unfamiliar with the idea of being tied for the night.

Lilly, still in adventure mode, lunged herself at a brisk walk around the tree until she reached the end of her rope. She then would turn and lunge herself the other direction. This worked until she somehow got her foot over the rope and then she would stand there with wide eyes looking for "mommy" to come and rescue her.

Q was even worse. She was the bossy mare and couldn't deal with Lilly's high energy at the end of the day when all she wanted to do was eat and rest. Q was big and she knew it and had little respect for her lead rope. Although she was very well behaved most of the time, and perfectly capable to stand tied for hours after polo or while we took a lunch break at a gas station, for some reason today wasn't her day. She pulled back on the rope, bracing herself against the tree, her front legs thrashing as she tried to free herself.

We leapt to her side to sooth her and she stopped immediately, as if unaware that she had been this close to breaking her lead rope buckle and being set free next to a busy road. We stroked her and she settled, though we couldn't blame her. A hurricane was approaching. It had been all over the news. We had hoped that in light of the situation at least SOMEONE would feel sorry enough for us to allow us shelter for the evening.

I had been on the verge of giving up, but Q and Lilly's obvious distress at being tied all night to a big tree gave me the courage for one last attempt. The sun was fading behind the mountains and soon it would be too dark to go anywhere. This was our last hope.

I posted on Facebook.

The power of social media proved itself that night and we found ourselves scrambling to saddle up with all our gear in record time. We had whittled our morning packing routine to about 2 and a half hours, but somehow, we managed to strap everything on as dusk fell.

We knew we were at risk heading out in low light, but we had no choice. We wore our reflective gear and mounted up. We had spent the past three weeks walking, but tonight, saddlebags and all, we trotted.

We arrived at our safe haven in the dark and were greeted by a woman with the friendliest smile. She showed our horses to their home for the night and led us to an empty horse stall where we could sleep through the storm. Her name was Sinéad and we couldn't thank her enough for coming to our rescue.

"Don't be silly, it's no trouble at all!"

She offered us the chance to stay an extra night so we could wait out the hurricane in safety. After our scare that day we decided to accept her kindness and enjoyed a day of rest and the chance to restock on our supplies.

Four Weeks In.

"I know you two must be tired, but would you like to come with me to a party tonight? It's an equestrian friend of mine's party because her homebred horse won at a recent show, so it will be horse people. And there will be plenty of food and there's an open bar..." Aoife added for good measure.

Aoife was our host for the night and had kindly allowed us into her beautiful home, all because of a friendly woman in the horse community by the name of Emma. Emma had been following our adventures online and we planned to head to meet her after our stay with Aoife.

Christian and I smiled, excited for an evening out. "Of course! Sounds fun," I said enthusiastically—not because of the open bar, but because of the break in our daily routine.

We had encountered several horrible, unpleasant days leading up to Aoife's. Not only were we going to bed just as soggy and wet as we were waking up in the morning, but we even had two occasions where during our ride the skies had opened and the hail began. We had no other options but to stop in the middle of the road as our horse's turned their tails to the hail. They nibbled on the grass on the roadside happily while Christian and I took most of the pelts from the hail on our backs. Even our large ponchos couldn't protect us from the bruises.

To top it off, I couldn't remember the last time I had slept in an actual bed. Aiofe had not only sorted our horses with two stalls full of fluffy bedding and a nice meal, but she delivered the same for us. I could have cried when I saw the fluffy pillows and guest room she had tidied up for our stay.

And now a party! What luck!

We did our best to clean up, adorning our nicest clothes—and by nicest, I mean washed—before heading out. We arrived at the party and realized very quickly it was quite posh. Thankfully it was indeed a room full of horse-people and Christian and I circulated the room enjoying the evening conversations with a variety of people.

It was fun having a chance to talk about our adventure and mishaps as if it wasn't currently happening to us. After all, our pal Emma had hooked us up with a place to stay for the next five nights and we wouldn't need to knock on random doors until Thursday.

What a relief!

Five Weeks In.

It seemed only fitting on our cross-Ireland adventure that eventually we meet a fox hunter. We were welcomed inside by Liam, our host for the evening. He had already given us a tour of his stables and introduced us to his big, strong fox hunting horses whom he adored. His two daughters and wife greeted us at the door and sat with us at the table for dinner.

Liam was bright and enthusiastic as he regaled us with stories about his years leading the local fox hunting troop. "In twenty years," he boasted, "we've never caught a fox. In fact, we don't want to, it's not really about the fox. But it's a lot of fun going on a hunt, you should join me for this weekend's hunt! The season has just started."

Christian's eyes lit up. I had to remind him that he had never jumped before except very small jumps in an arena and wasn't quite yet ready for galloping and jumping big jumps on big horses. Admittedly, I was a show jumper and although I loved big jumps on big horses, the idea of solid walls and big dykes and ditches made me more than a little nervous.

"You can jump with the ponies," Liam pointed to his two teenage daughters. "They take their Connemara ponies on the hunts and sometimes I think the ponies are better than the big horses the way they climb over every obstacle."

Liam's wife, Katelyn, was equally enthusiastic to share stories and we sat in awe as they told us about their trip to Connemara with their horses and how they befriended a local and had to navigate a marsh.

Just when we thought the evening of story-telling couldn't get any better, we were led into the dining with a warm cozy fire. "Our girls are going to perform for you," Katelyn grinned, egging her daughters on with an encouraging nod.

"Yes!" Liam clapped, "they are both excellent Irish dancers, musicians and singers! We believe it's very important to keep our traditions and culture alive so they will play for you some traditional Irish instruments and then dance for you."

I was stunned. "Really?" Hadn't I just been talking to Christian about that the other day, how I wanted to see some local dancing before the end of our trip? Remembering what it was like being a teenager with talent (though mine had been specifically horses) I turned to the two teens. "Is that ok? Do you mind?" I asked their permission, not wanting to be the cause for them missing out on an evening of... well whatever it is teenage girls do these days.

"It's ok, they make us do this kind of stuff all the time," a hint of teen angst could be seen as she rolled her eyes. They began playing us instruments and Liam joined in with the singing.

"You're a bum
You're a punk
You're an old slut on junk
Lying there almost dead on a drip in that bed
You scumbag, you maggot
You cheap lousy faggot

Happy Christmas your arse
I pray God it's our last..."

The girls didn't seem that annoyed to play for us as they giggled while he continued to sing. Christian and I were laughing, I tried my best not to tear up. After the song had finished the girls swapped instruments. I couldn't keep up with the talent of these two. The number of musical instruments combined with their singing and Irish dancing, complete with floor stomping, put me in a trance of wonderment.

When they had finished and were able to return to eye rolling again, they delicately returned their dancing shoes and instruments. "You see that photo hanging there on the wall," Katelyn motioned at the beautiful painting overlooking the den. The picture was of a man with a fiddle riding a horse at night. A path lay before them, leading them to the large house with lit rooms in the distance.

"Yes," I nodded.

"Ireland has a rich tradition of storytelling in our history. The Celtic culture has been passing down these stories for over 2,000 years. In the old days, these story tellers would wander from place to place. They belonged nowhere, and were travelers offering their stories in exchange for a warm bed or food. They entertained the people and kept our history and culture alive. It's important that we remember to honor these travelers and storytellers, and to keep the traditions alive."

I blinked, my eyes lost in the painting. I had always wondered about my Irish roots. Growing up in California I had been raised with the "American version" of my Irish heritage and had no connections to who my original ancestors were before coming to the States. Coming to Ireland had been a calling of mine since I was little and looking at that lone rider on his horse, about to knock on a door and offer his stories in exchange for a meal and a bed I couldn't help but breathe a sigh of relief.

We had become a herd, the four of us. We had ridden through downtown city centers on a weekend, taking advantage of the staring passerby's as we left the one-way street and casually strolled down a "pedestrian only" lane. We had survived sourcing not one but FOUR farriers during our ride to replace a lost shoe or fit them with a new set. (The hard road surfaces caused them to grind their shoes into dust after only about a week and a half.)

We had the privilege of meeting countless strangers and leaving with a friend or near-family member within the space of an evening. We had witnessed kindness without expectation, helpfulness without greediness and patches of sunshine amid a hailstorm.

And more importantly, without even realizing it, in a fading Irish tradition, slowly being replaced by cell phones, busy highways, and Google... we brought the tradition of storytelling back to life.

Thank You For Reading!

Dear Reader,

I hope you enjoyed this 1st installment in the Equestrian Adventuresses Book Series. I have to tell you, I love stories from adventuresses just like you. If you crave more stories like these, fear not, we will be back in Book 5 of the Series. As an author, I love feedback. I have received many messages from readers thanking me for this series for inspiring them to travel on horseback and take a chance.

You are the reason I will keep seeking stories from amazing Equestrian Adventuresses. Please let us know what you liked, loved and even what you hated. I'd love to hear from you. You can email me at www.equestrianadventuresses.com or post in our Facebook Group.

I need to ask a favor. If your so inclined, I'd love it if you would post a review on Amazon. Loved it, hated it—I'd just like to hear your feedback. Reviews can be tough to come by these days, and you, the reader, have the power to make or break a book. If you have the time, here's a link to my author page, along with all my books on amazon: www.amazon.com/author/krystal-kelly

Thank you so much for reading *Saddles and Sisterhood,* and for spending time with me. I look forward to many more adventures together in the future!

In Gratitude,
Krystal Kelly
Equestrian Adventuresses Founder

About Equestrian Adventuresses

Equestrian Adventuresses was founded in 2019 as a community for women who love horses, travel and adventure. You can listen to more inspirational stories from real women's travels on horseback on the podcast show available on iTunes, Spotify, Stitcher and more. You can also find a variety of travel documentaries on:

YouTube Channel:
www.youtube.com/c/equestrianadventuresses as well as read short stories and find helpful resources on the website:

www.equestrianadventuresses.com

Join the community and check out the Facebook Group: EquestrianAdventuresses

Other Books by Equestrian Adventuresses:

Equestrian Adventuresses Series

Book 1: Saddles and Sisterhood
Book 2: Going the Distance
Book 3: Leg Up
Book 4: Have Breeches Will Travel

Travel Guide for Equestrians Series

Best in 2020 World Travel Guide
Best in 2020 USA Travel Guide
2021 Job Book - How to Work Abroad with
Horses
Horse Riding in Every Country Catalog: A Catalog of 400+ Riding Opportunities in Over 180+
Countries

*Download your FREE E-Books here:
www.EquestrianAdventuresses.com

Coming Soon!
Equestrian Adventuresses Book 5

Dreaming of Traveling the World on Horseback but Don't Know Where to Start?

Introducing the **Equestrian Adventuresses Online Courses,** the first ever online home-study courses that gives you the necessary confidence and skills to become an equestrian adventuress.

What you'll learn:
- How to Speak the Horse Language in ANY country
- How to be more confident on the ground and in the saddle with horses
- How to travel solo confidently
- Strategies to achieve your goals--no matter how big your dreams are
- How to gain your horse's trust and build their confidence
- Mastering your own body language
- What is "Energy" and how does it influence your horse
- How to stay safe while traveling as a solo woman
- How to read situations

- Effective strategies to turn your goals, ideas & dreams into ACTIONABLE PLANS
- And much, much more!

For more information check out the Equestrian Adventuresses Online Courses Here:
www.EquestrianAdventuresses.com

About the Author
Ciska Vandenhaute

Ciska Vandenhaute is a Belgian rider and has been an equestrian adventuress since childhood. Growing from Welsh ponies to thoroughbreds, she has been riding almost her entire life. A few years back, she discovered trail riding abroad together with her mom and they have been hooked ever since, never letting a year go by without going on journeys on horseback together. Follow her adventures on: travelsthroughtheears on instagram!
https://www.instagram.com/travelsthroughtheears/

About the Author
Danielle Haslam

Danielle Haslam is known as being "pony mad" and obsessed with travel. She has ridden Quarter horses in the American west, Icelandic's over lava fields, Arabians across deserts, Andalusians down beaches and done dressage on Lusitanos. When she is not daydreaming about her next trip, she can usually be found exploring the countryside on Paddy her beloved skewbald cob. She lives in a cottage in Yorkshire, with her husband Luke and their three cats. My Canadian Hero: An Encounter with Bears is her first published story.

About the Author
Jeannette Polowski

Jeannette Polowski is an adventurous woman who resides in New York State. She has had a lifelong love of all animals, especially horses. Married for 26 years, she has 4 daughters and 2 grandchildren. When not working full time in healthcare, she enjoys spending time with her family, pets and living life to its fullest.

About the Author
Sandra Kelly

Sandra Kelly was born in Northern California near San Francisco. She spent her early years living there until she was eleven and her family moved to the Sierra Nevada Mountains near Lake Tahoe. Having so much more room to roam she developed her love for the outdoors. She is a retired Agent from the California Department of Justice, has two kids and currently lives in Colorado. She is now an Equestrian Adventuress, author, mentor and business woman.

About the Author
Krystal Kelly

Krystal Kelly is founder of Equestrian Adventuresses and an avid traveler on a quest to visit every country in the world. She left her home in California at the age of 21 to work abroad with top show jumping horses. She has since worked in over 20 countries with horses including Egypt, India, Romania, and many others. In 2016 she met her husband while driving a crappy car from England to Mongolia and back. Her love of adventurous travel has led her to the farthest corners of the Earth to film for the Equestrian Adventuresses Documentary series, bringing her husband along for the ride to capture the beauty on film.

www.equestrianadventuresses.com

**Enjoyed this book?
Please leave a review
ON AMAZON!**

Printed in Great Britain
by Amazon